ALL IS NOT LOST

Words of comfort,
hope and healing
for handling life's
toug~

D1166486

ALL IS NOT LOST

The Healing Journey
Through
Crisis, Grief and Loss

C. Leslie Charles

Books and products by C. Leslie Charles
are distributed by Yes! Press.
Quantity discounts are available.

Yes!Press

PO Box 956
East Lansing, MI 48826
517.675.7535
www.LeslieCharles.com

Cover Design by Diana L. Grinwis
Cover Photo by Allison Eastin

ISBN 0-9644621-3-3

Printed in the United States of America
2 3 4 5 6 7 8 9 10

To my son Robbie,
whose life was far too short.

TABLE OF CONTENTS

ACKNOWLEDGMENTS

My everlasting gratitude goes first to Rob, my loving life partner, editor, publisher, and much more. Thank you, Carol Mase, for reading and commenting on the manuscript and Mary Bradshaw, for your feedback when the book was in its embryonic stage.

Thank you also to Ruth Lucas, Barbara Glanz, Chris Sharpe, Antoinette Imhoff, Ann Brandt, Donna Bohannan, Sam and Wanda Rieger, Debbie Parnam, Loretta Win, Maggie Bedrosian, W Mitchell, Marta Varee Pearson, Debby Buck DeJonge, Segami, Chuck Cote, Eddie Leigh, Denise Taylor-McGinn, Craig Smith, Mary McDaniel, Emory Austin, Janie Jason, Joan Morgan, Judy McQueen, and Renee Lagala.

Last but not least, thank you, Susan RoAne and Sam Horn for your friendship and ongoing encouragement. I wouldn't be the writer I am without you two.

Were it not for times of darkness
we would never see the stars.

INTRODUCTION

While most of us share a common desire for happiness, success, and peace of mind, there are other aspects of life we'd rather not have to deal with. Death. Divorce. Disappointment. Illness. Sadness. Tragedy. Hurt. There are points in your life and mine where we will face loss, whether it involves the end of a relationship or job, illness or accident, betrayal, financial hardship, death of a beloved person or pet, letting go of a long held dream, or a massive national tragedy.

Experiencing emotional pain is an intensely personal process. It's common to feel alone, isolated, and disconnected from others. In our efforts to heal it's sometimes hard to know where to begin picking up the pieces. If you are recovering from a loss, I hope the ideas in this book will bring comfort to your aching soul, give you a sense of what you're in for, and offer some healthy ways to handle your hurt so you can move forward in your life.

If you have lost a loved one you'll find words of comfort and hope that will help ease your hurt and give you the strength to heal. If you are recovering from the distress of divorce you'll discover some insights that can help you adjust, and eventually, thrive in your new life. If you have lost your job or feel as if you're stuck in a period of confusion or angst, you will find some ideas that will help you break free.

I had never planned on writing a book like this but following the September 11 tragedy I couldn't stop thinking about the thousands of people whose lives had been so dramatically altered in a single morning. Having experienced the sudden death of my youngest son, I know the feeling of having my world turned on its side at a moment's notice.

One unique aspect of September 11 was its universality. Our shared sense of shock, bewilderment, and outrage brought us together. Those of us who were not directly affected by the attacks identified with those who were. As a nation, we grieved, knowing that things would never be the same. Such is the nature of loss.

Yet life goes on, and while this book explores the painful, difficult side of existence it's also a tribute to the resilience of the human spirit. Even in the aftermath of loss, crisis, or trauma, we somehow find ways to prevail. This book is about what you can expect as you progress from floundering in the depths of despair to healing your heart and spirit so you can once again soar with all you believe in.

If you have recently suffered a significant loss or setback in your life, even though it doesn't feel like it at this moment, please believe that all is not lost. You will recover. You will once again find sense and meaning in your life. Even though grief and sadness set us apart from others for a time, we are not quite as alone as we may feel. There is much to draw from: comfort from those who care about us, the inner resource of our own resilience, and the strength that comes from all we care about and believe in.

How we express our spirituality is as intensely personal as how we handle crisis or grief, and for this reason I have intentionally left room for you to interject the tenets of your faith or spiritual beliefs rather than impose my own. Healing requires the full involvement of mind, body, and spirit, and each of us must find our path and follow it in our own way, step by step, along the foreign terrain of the healing journey.

The Healing Journey

Chapter I
MY JOURNEY

It was September 9, 1984 when my son Robbie's life came to an end. He was twenty-one years old and the youngest of my three children. Robbie sustained a fatal injury in the last hour of his night shift on the oil rig where he worked in central Michigan. My son was already dead by the time we were notified, which meant none of us had a chance to say goodbye. In one brief phone call, my life, and the lives of my ex husband and our two surviving children were changed forever.

Like every other parent who has lost a child, I never dreamed anything like this would happen to me. My kids, athletic and healthy, grew into adulthood without suffering as much as a broken bone or major illness and for this I had always felt blessed.

All Is Not Lost

When people find out about my son's death, they ask how I could have survived such a loss. My answer is, "Sometimes I wonder, too. I simply did." And in a way it's true. As many others have done, I just went on, day after day, working through my grief, putting my life back together, and learning what I could from the experience, one small step at a time.

Monitoring my progress was quite an education. I learned that I, just like others I have either known or read about, have an enormous capacity for recovery. Somehow, some way, slowly, we heal. Giving up simply isn't an option. Recovering from loss is a perfect example of living one day at a time. Despite our pain, we move on and begin reordering our world.

We never forget the experience, but in time we learn to recall that period without having to relive all of the pain. I have thought about my son almost every day since his death and I've come to peace with my loss. Did it take time? Of course. The path of healing is long and slow, over rough, uncertain ground. But by picking our way carefully and refusing to quit, we find our way to acceptance.

Regardless of our loss we will sometimes come in contact with those who have endured even more, and they can be a source of inspiration. At Robbie's funeral, a former neighbor came up to me, a mother of four who had lost not one, but two of her young adult children, in two separate accidents a few years apart. Ruth hugged me and said, "It may not feel like it at this moment, but time does heal." She was right.

If you have survived a painful loss you know exactly what Ruth was talking about. For me, time did its work, just like she said, and I held up my side of the bargain, too. I found that recovering from grief is a series of conscious, deliberate choices, a daily acknowledgment that while things will never be the same, life does go on. With this loss as a part of my history, I have grown stronger, fortified all that I believe in, and expanded my awareness about what really matters. In time, the same will happen with you.

Chapter 2
LIVING WITH LOSS

Life brings us joy and fulfillment, and it also brings sorrow and crisis. As children we amass the scars of private hurts, losses, and traumas, some of which stay with us as we grow up. Once we become adults we have new challenges, losses, and letdowns to bear and when a crisis strikes, some of those old wounds might resurface and magnify our hurt. Because we live in a land where the pursuit of happiness is considered an inalienable right, most of us are pitifully unprepared for grief or loss.

When crisis occurs, whether on a personal scale

such as death, divorce, and job loss, or a far reaching magnitude such as natural disasters or acts of war, we immediately try to make sense of what has happened. As our minds vainly search for reasons and explanations, sometimes we find the answers we so desperately seek, but other times we find nothing. This is a time for faith and hope. It's also a time to draw upon our innate strength, wisdom, and spiritual resources for comfort so we can go on.

Despite the hurt it brings, loss can teach us rich lessons about life, love, and our capacity to find new meaning. People constantly tell me that with their losses came new levels of understanding and clarification they would otherwise never have discovered. If you are currently in a state of grief this may be hard to imagine, but I encourage you to hang onto these hopeful thoughts. In the meantime, let the grieving and healing do their work over time.

The deeper your loss, the more it hurts. The

more you hurt, the more you need to retreat, reflect, and heal. Our culture allows little time or space for such indulgences but I urge you to take what you need.

Whether a loss is instant and unexpected, or gradual and anticipated, it provokes feelings of isolation and disconnectedness because it is so very personal. Only you fully comprehend the extent of the hurt, loss, or letdown you feel. It may feel as if you're on an emotional roller coaster; completely calm one moment and out of control the next. This is not unusual.

Time may seem suspended in your world while everything else keeps rushing by. It may feel as if you are viewing things through a haze, numbed to what's happening around you. Little things that mattered yesterday may not even register today and vice versa; what seemed inconsequential a short time ago can now feel almost overwhelming in its significance.

When a loved one dies it feels as if every cell in your body is affected, and truth be told, that's exactly

The Healing Journey

what happens. When her son died from cancer, my friend Ann talked about feeling drained, describing in detail the effort it took to simply go through the motions of getting dressed, eating, and performing everyday tasks. Yet, as the months have passed, life has gotten easier for her. Slowly but surely, her heart has begun to heal.

When a loved one dies, society expects us to stop, withdraw, and pull away from the mainstream, but only for a brief period. With divorce, we are somehow expected to keep on with our lives, working, socializing, and tending to everyday matters as if we had nothing else on our mind. Because our way of life leaves so little room for resolving our emotional losses, many of us never fully heal.

Divorce or the end of a long term relationship is a loss that brings feelings of alienation, disappointment, and anger, and possibly embarrassment, guilt, or a sense of failure. For a time, our mixed emotions congeal into a heavy weight that we just can't shake.

All Is Not Lost

A full time homemaker whose husband of twenty years decided to call it quits was nearly immobilized with grief. She and her husband had a comfortable life and three great kids but he decided it wasn't enough. There was no affair, he just wanted out.

Having acceded to his desire that she devote her time to her family instead of a career, Bonnie felt bitter and resentful about his decision to end the marriage. Knowing I had lost a child, Bonnie said she would rather endure a death than a demoralizing divorce like this one. She helped me realize that when a loved one dies, we grieve for them. When we divorce or end a significant relationship, we grieve for ourselves.

A Healing Step

Loss slices life into two dimensions: Before and after. Then and now. It may feel as if your heartache will never go away but it does subside with time. Despite your hurt, take comfort in other people's compassion, bolster yourself with purpose, and seek solace in your spirituality. The deeper you look, the more there is to discover. Although the process is tedious and demanding, you will find the tender mercies of healing as you go.

Structure can offer a welcome haven during times of pain, especially following the death of a loved one. After Robbie's death, I found that the ritual of having to get up, get dressed, and be somewhere (at the funeral home) to do something (receive visitors) gave me a mission. I considered these activities a blessing because there was nothing else I could have done at the time.

Whether you are recovering from a death, divorce or other hurt, in times of grieving try to follow some of your personal rituals and daily activities even if it feels as if you are simply going through the motions. I don't mean push yourself relentlessly. If you need to just sit and think, or cry, do it. But it often helps to follow some of your usual patterns: Get out of bed. Clean up. Get dressed. Eat something, even if you don't feel like it. Walk the dog. Organize a closet or other space. Write in your journal. Shine your shoes. Dust. Mindless chores can be a welcome diversion for an aching heart.

From everyday tasks to the later significant activities of putting away memorabilia or sorting through personal effects, structure gives you somewhere to go and something to do instead of circling in your grief.

The end of a marriage or long term relationship requires similar steps, such as sorting through and splitting up property, changing or updating legal agreements, rearranging your physical surroundings to accommodate new empty spaces, and readjusting your daily patterns now that you're on your own. Let structure be your companion as you take your first steps on the path toward healing.

The Healing Journey

Take especially good care of yourself during the early days. Accept the support and encouragement offered by compassionate friends. Read the passages in this book you find the most comforting. Commit to moving on despite your pain. Time is your ally. It will help you find peace. Let it work for you. You've heard the words a thousand times, "This too, shall pass," and they ring with truth. Hold onto those words.

Chapter 3
THE DIVIDING LINE

Grief and loss take us to inward places we may never have visited before; places that feel uncomfortable and unfamiliar. As your world splits into "before and after," it's common to feel alone and separate from others, whether you're surrounded by people who care about what you're going through, or if your loss is invisible to all but you.

For a time you will see the world differently. Your senses will be keener. You'll take things more personally. You'll be more susceptible to frustration and more sensitive to what people say or do. This is because you've crossed the dividing line that separates you from others. Don't worry, at some point that line will disappear and you'll return to the mainstream. But while you're there it helps to understand how this dividing line affects you.

The first and most obvious change is in language, where verbs shift from present tense to past: from "is" to "was." It feels unnatural and awkward at first, a painful reminder of the massive change your life has undergone. In losing a loved one (person or pet), or after divorce, you will find yourself talking in present tense, momentarily forgetting that things have changed. Then you catch yourself, making the switch to past tense.

The Healing Journey

This adjustment is one of the first steps of acceptance. There are social divisions too, and they're not as easily controlled as our own language because they involve other people. It seems that we human beings, in our desire to maintain an orderly, predictable world, are inclined to draw distinctions. Just like neatly tracing a line down the middle of a page, we distinguish between the married and unmarried, the parents and the childless, the ill and the well, the unemployed and the employed, the living and the dead, and so on.

Consider the workplace dividing line between those who lose their job or get demoted and those who are still safely at their desks. Or how an illness or physical condition divides the able bodied from the disabled. The diagnosis of a chronic illness immediately separates you or your loved one from those who are well.

Even losing a pet can mean losing your connection with other cat or dog lovers, or in my case, horse owners. And so on. Even if it's not of your choosing, the circumstance that puts you on the other side of the social dividing line can also lead to additional, unanticipated losses and it can be lonely over there.

My friend Barbara who lost her husband after thirty-three years of marriage was hurt and stunned when long time friends (couples) quit inviting her to parties and social functions. She couldn't believe that the same people she regarded as close friends had left her behind because she was no longer part of a couple. So it isn't just life's inevitable losses we must reckon with, but also their unexpected consequences.

There are additional complications for those who divorce. A newly separated woman may now be perceived as a threat by her married friends who worry that their husbands might be tempted to stray. A suddenly single man's compliment to a female friend may be interpreted as a come on. Like it or not, after a divorce, one's new social status moves the line of scrimmage and changes the game.

The Healing Journey

As if it isn't enough to go through the trauma of divorce and the attending regrets or insecurities that come along with it, you also have to contend with other people's insecurities, too. This can make for lonely times because not only do you lose a partner, you may also lose some of your social ties, particularly from those friendships that tacitly require its members to come in pairs. Just like my widowed friend Barbara, your once solid social structure may undergo an unexpected shift.

A Healing Step

Remembering that our culture does little to prepare us for grief and loss, most of us aren't even aware of the dividing line, let alone how to support or comfort someone on the other side. If there's a book of grief etiquette, I've never seen it. In other words, we are at a loss as to how loss should be handled, whether it's our own or someone else's.

All Is Not Lost

When you experience a crisis, some people simply won't know how to express their sympathy because they're not clear on their role. Some friends won't know if they should mention your loss and risk upsetting you, or if they should simply avoid it. You'll help yourself if you can lay some of your expectations aside.

I know, this is asking you to be strong when you least feel like it. Chances are, a radical change in your life and lifestyle means you may lose some friends along the way. But if you accept that people who care about you may be experiencing their own feelings of helplessness and loss, you'll experience less disappointment and maybe a few pleasant surprises.

Close friends who seem backed off simply may not know how to help at first. Give them time. Recognizing that some people will feel awkward and unsure can ease your feelings of separation. Those who truly care about you don't like your being on the other side of that dividing line either. If you sense that a friend or loved one is struggling with how to comfort you, initiate a conversation so they know it's okay to talk about things.

If you have children, please understand that they too have crossed a dividing line. You'll need to talk with them. Don't wait for them to approach you. They may not say anything because they're afraid, or may not know what to ask. Just as you need comfort and support, your children may need an abundance of reassurance.

If you find yourself feeling lonely, realize that you are probably not be the only one. If nothing else, keep a watchful eye out for how your kids are doing and do your best to be there for them. Your time with them may ease some of the loneliness and separateness you all feel.

But don't be a martyr. Let yourself be helped or comforted by those who offer. We're not encouraged to be "takers" in this culture and it can be hard accepting someone's help. Figuring that you've had many occasions to be the giver (and that the giving side of the dividing line is easier for you), now is an appropriate time for you to be the receiver. Keep in mind that by graciously accepting offers of comfort or assistance you allow others to be the giver.

Understanding the social dividing line may enable you to cope with the isolation you feel when going through an upheaval. It may also help you more effectively comfort a friend or loved when they find themselves on the other side. Goodness knows, as our world becomes less predictable and more uncertain, we could all benefit by making that social dividing line as narrow as possible.

The Healing Journey

Chapter 4
WHY ME?

When bad things happen, it's tempting to ask why. But sometimes there simply isn't an answer, and asking this question may only increase our anguish. I recognize there are many people who believe everything happens for a reason or that it's simply God's will and if this is your position I respect that.

My position is that events, isolated acts, and large scale tragedies simply occur, sometimes for reasons, sometimes not. If our culture were less insulated and paid more attention to world events we would have a much more complete picture of the suffering, insults, and hardships that occur every day on this planet.

As for our personal lives, I believe we have a responsibility to try and make sense of whatever hap-

All Is Not Lost

pens to us in the best way we can; that it's our job to find the lesson, insight, and sometimes even the blessing embedded in the pain so we can incorporate it into the whole of our life as we move on.

Some years ago I read an article about a woman whose adolescent daughter was kidnapped, raped, and killed, the most horrific situation any parent could endure. I was touched by her steadfast refusal to ask why her daughter had been brutalized. This courageous mother went on to explain that she didn't ask why because she feared that if she began asking, she would never stop. Her resolve helped me resist asking why my son had to die at such a tender age and under such traumatic circumstances (he didn't die instantly).

The Buddhist monk Thich Nhat Hanh came to a place of inner peace and resolution in the face of unspeakable atrocities, as did Holocaust survivor Viktor Frankl. Instead of asking why, each of these individuals looked for, and found meaning and purpose in their

The Healing Journey

lives. They prevailed in spite of their experiences and resolved to help others do the same. I find the choices they made and the messages in their books both rational and inspiring.

So for me, the question has become "why ask why?" When wonderful things happen, consider how few people ask why. Imagine a Super Lotto winner lying awake night after night, fitful and tortured, asking, "Why me?" My point, of course, is that if we don't ask this question when good things happen, why ask it about the bad? Asking why opens a gate that may unleash a flood of remorse, frustration, anger, and feelings of powerlessness.

I won't suggest you're wrong if you do so, but consider that asking "why" is different from asking "how." The latter might offer factual information or explanations, but asking why can expose you to more self-inflicted pain than you bargained for, or deserve.

A divorce, even an amicable one, can provoke a

succession of questions, second guessing and conjecture. How did we come to this? Was splitting up truly the best option? Did we try hard enough? Should we have stayed together even though there was so little left between us? Am I making a mistake? My brother Bob married and divorced the same woman twice to answer such questions.

After years of working doggedly and fighting (literally) to maintain our connection, my life partner Rob and I enjoy a relationship that spans nearly three decades. On at least three occasions we nearly broke up, but chose to work things out instead. At the time, splitting up would have been easier.

I am an advocate of counseling and communication or relationship maintenance classes to help couples keep from drifting apart. But if divorce is the best option, as it was for my ex husband and me, then there's a point where we need to put our issues to rest and move forward.

The Healing Journey

Of course, some questions will go unanswered. Resolution may come but closure may not. And yes, it's human nature to want answers or seek closure, but there's no guarantee that's what we'll get, either with divorce or death.

My friend and client Lori lost her brother under questionable circumstances and the police were unable to determine whether his death was murder or suicide. Sadly, her family must find a way to live with the ambiguity of never knowing for sure, and there are countless people in similar circumstances. Families who lose a loved one through suicide or an act of violence tell me that closure does not exist for them. There exists a part of their hurt that will never heal, yet even these stalwart souls find ways of moving on.

One woman I know whose daughter committed suicide is writing a book about her experience to help others deal with their grief, guilt, and helplessness. In Arizona, two mothers whose teen aged sons were

All Is Not Lost

killed in separate incidents have dedicated their lives to educating "at risk" teens and families about options other than violence, drugs, and aggression in the hope of preventing more tragedies like theirs.

Sam and Wanda Rieger, whose daughter Melanie was killed by her boyfriend in a fit of rage established an annual conference, Survivors of Homicide, in their daughter's name. I'm touched by their commitment to not only survive their heartbreaking ordeal, but to help others who may one day face similar circumstances.

Having briefly visited the world of those whose loved ones have died as a result of violence reminded me that no matter how much I may hurt, there is someone, somewhere, hurting even more. I learned that survivors of violence not only suffer a gruesome loss, but they find themselves frustrated by unsympathetic, unresponsive social and legal systems that often add to, rather than relieve their anguish.

The Healing Journey

Sadly, in our culture we don't make much room for handling the messy business of life, particularly, intense emotional pain or physical suffering. And though it doesn't invade all people's lives, there are many families who must cope with the aftermath of suicide or violence.

From large scale horrors such as Oklahoma City and September 11 to isolated incidents most of us never hear about, people sometimes do horrible things to themselves or each other. What I find most regrettable is that in the case of suicide, we often never know why. As for murder, sometimes it's done for no reason. No reason at all. Ask the killers why and they have no answer. If they can't explain why, how can we?

A Healing Step

When life hands you loss, tragedy, or times of suffering, resist adding to your load. Instead of feeling

All Is Not Lost

singled out or picked on, remind yourself that hard times are a part of everyone's life and at some point we will each be exposed. If the issue you're struggling with is a terminal illness, I recommend *Kitchen Table Wisdom* by Rachel Naomi Remen, a touching and tremendously inspiring book.

Granted, some losses are more extreme than others, yet even the taxing ones can be life transforming. When you are in period of loss or grieving, remind yourself that pain and wisdom are distant ends of the same thread. As the hurt begins to subside, it will be replaced with comfort and meaning.

Pain and insight, loss and discovery, turmoil and peace are all intricately woven into the same fabric. The closer we look at life, the more texture we find. It's not a question of why, but how. A Buddhist might say it this way: Things happen. We wake up. We go on.

My hope is that if or when your life is touched by sadness or loss, instead of asking why, you'll ask what you can take away from this experience as a means of comforting yourself. Perhaps what you find will also, in some way, help you provide comfort for someone who hasn't yet learned the tough lesson of not asking why.

Chapter 5
YOU JUST NEVER KNOW

When you experience a crisis you may observe strange and unpredictable behaviors in those around you, from obsessive attention to outright avoidance. Those you consider good friends may disappear while mere acquaintances shower you with support and encouragement. You just never know, but one thing seems certain: facing a crisis is hard on everyone because nobody knows exactly what to do.

Some years ago one of my horseback riding pals

was temporarily disabled after being thrown. Not only had nerve damage rendered one of her arms useless for months, she also walked with a severe limp due to a fractured vertebrae. While she was incapacitated, Tori's other "stable" friends avoided her. I remember taking her out to dinner and even cutting the meat on her plate while the others stayed away.

Maybe they were afraid that being so close to someone who had been hurt by a horse would rub off on them. Considering how much time we all spent together socially, I was unable to comprehend how Tori's friends vanished during her convalescence.

Earlier I mentioned my friend Barbara who, after her husband's death, discovered she was no longer a part of the small society they had enjoyed. Married friends with whom they had socialized for more than twenty years began leaving her out. Now that she is widowed and single, Barbara no longer fits in a "couples" circle.

The Healing Journey

Although I experienced similar treatment after my divorce many years ago, I was disappointed that social desertion would happen to a widow, too. Sadly, when Barbara most needed the company of her friends, many of them were no longer there for her. If you're recently divorced this may help you feel more prepared in case some of your friends behave in similar fashion.

If you're recently separated but were never married, there's another consideration. When a friend of mine ended a nine year relationship with her life partner she discovered that couples who live together rather than marry often experience an absence of condolences when they break up. Even close friends often don't treat the dissolution of a long term relationship as they would the end of a marriage, even though both newly separated parties experience the same disappointment or sense of loss.

People who suffer a long term debilitating illness frequently experience a gradual drop off of friends and acquaintances. My cousin Chris, a gifted athlete who was diagnosed with muscular dystrophy as an adult has struggled to maintain his strength and agility, but as his condition has changed, so has his peer group. This is pretty typical. As one's disease progresses and physical abilities decline, friends and relatives are less inclined to hang around, finding it uncomfortable and inconvenient being in the company of someone whose mobility is compromised.

There's also the emotional distress of witnessing the slow physical (or mental) deterioration of someone they care about. Certainly this is one of the many burdens that caregivers experience on a day to day basis, not to mention the social isolation that comes with caring for another.

My friend Judy whose husband has Alzheimer's is still able to leave him while she goes to her full time job, but things are changing. Judy says it feels as if she's saying goodbye to him in degrees, and in many ways, she is. Similarly, my friend Maggie watched her mother slowly succumb to the disease. Maggie once described how her mother's eyes lit up at a colorful necklace of numbers worn by her daughter-in-law, an elementary teacher. Maggie's mother touched the beads, saying with delight, "One, two, three, blue!"

I've watched my father's mental faculties fade and his dependency on my mother increase since his colon cancer surgery nearly two years ago. Both of them are coping with their own frustrations and private grief over his lost capacity and some of it gets expressed as anger. Caregiving is such a cluster of loss unto itself, on so many levels, and based on my observations, until it's time for hospice, options for outside support seem pitifully lacking.

The oncologist has never offered any speculation as to dad's diminished mental skills nor does he directly address mom's other questions. Since dad's first chemo appointment, few of the oncology staff have shown an inclination to inform, educate, or in any way support mom in her new caregiver role. Despite her questions and attempts to gain insights about dad's odd behaviors since his surgery, mom feels very left out.

I recently met a woman who has lived with multiple sclerosis for well over a decade. Many of Donna's former friends no longer come by and although this is typical, it's also a shame. Her old friend Carol still visits regularly, taking Donna on shopping excursions and other outings just as they always did, only with a few modifications.

These two friends still share their laughter, camaraderie, and memories. Carol has become the link between Donna's past and present, helping others grasp that Donna was once an extremely athletic woman who regularly enjoyed swimming, skiing, riding, and other sports.

My pal Antoinette is blessed with a solid group of friends who rallied after her stroke, modifying her house for a wheel chair and throwing a big welcome home party following her extended rehabilitation. Diane, a cancer patient, has a cadre of friends who built her a friendship "nest" consisting of memorabilia and tokens to reflect their ongoing love and support as she battles her disease. Yes, some people may bail out, but not all. Some friends are there for the duration.

❧

A Healing Step

We all react to crisis in our own personal way. Before my son's death I was less empathic than I am today, but I've learned that it takes very little effort to help someone else feel better. A quick phone call, a hand written note, or a greeting card convey acknowledgment and a desire to comfort.

I encourage you to review the times you've offered unconditional support to a friend who needed it, and maybe even those few times when you didn't. At the same time, reflect on those who are there for you and what this says about the relationships you share. If you have friends or loved ones who have consistently been there for you when you've needed them, send them blessings.

As you know, there will be people in your life who simply won't know how to handle your crisis, and their withdrawal can compound the grief you already feel. Even though this abandonment hurts, don't give it any more time than it deserves. It will be self-defeating to waste energy being angry at the people who let you down.

If they're gone, they're gone. You have healing work to do. Let them go, with as little anger or resentment as you can muster, so you can direct your energy into what you have some control over; the state of your own mind, body, and spirit.

Making the choice to take care of yourself is not selfish, though some may accuse you of that. Consider that the only time people call you selfish is when you aren't doing what they want you to. You can spell the word like this: self-ish. Self-affirming choices are a necessary step in your healing.

Sadly, we are not a particularly compassionate culture. Many of us are self-absorbed and impatient with others. Yet, we have the capacity to care. The outpouring of money, blood donations, and on site support from across our nation following September 11 illustrates that we have an amazing capacity for compassion when we try. Surviving your own crises and losses will increase your capacity for caring and it will also sensitize you to other people's struggles.

Perhaps one day, when something bad happens to a friend or loved one, their loss will bring out a level of compassion in you that you didn't even know you had. You just never know.

All Is Not Lost

Chapter 6

GETTING THROUGH THE "FIRSTS"

A major loss, particularly the death of a loved one, brings with it the issue of dealing with the "firsts": the first week, the first month, the first birthday or anniversary, holiday season, and occasions the two of you celebrated. Then there's the last "first," the one year anniversary of the date your world changed. Expect that your moods will fluctuate with the calendar, especially during the first year or two.

Physical reminders of a lost loved one can prompt an unexpected rush of emotions: a photograph, home video, item of clothing, a favorite chair in the living or dining room, even gazing at their side of the bed.

Loss of family pets can stir a sense of sadness

as you pass by the places and spaces they once occupied. Rob and I mourned the loss of our cat Ditto for a long time, especially when we walked by her favorite sleeping spot.

I know a woman who left her dog's dish on the floor for two months after he died to honor the memory of a pet that had been so much a part of the family. It certainly helps to take comfort where you can.

During the early days and months following a death you may find yourself experiencing momentary floods of intense pain, despair, or anguish with cascading memories, flashbacks, and fantasies about going back in time. The hopeful news is that these emotional rushes are typical of the early days and in time they taper off.

The first year after a separation or divorce may bring similar angst. If not huge waves of emotion, you may experience periods of depression or feelings of sorrow for what couldn't be, even if you know deep in your heart that you made the right decision.

All Is Not Lost

Children need time to cope, too. Sometimes we think that kids don't process emotions as deeply as we do, but they too, grieve. Children experience loss, though they may not have the words for it. They also have fewer coping mechanisms than we grown ups do. The better we understand that, the more we can be there for them.

You'll benefit from healthy rituals that ease your soul (journaling, praying, meditating, reading an inspirational passage when you need a lift, consciously recalling happy memories). Or you may need to express and process your grief physically. Cry if you feel sad, punch a pillow if you're angry. Exercise or go for a walk if you have excess energy or take a nap if you feel the need. Talk to your dead loved one if you're alone. Your modes of expression may change from day to day, so let your intuition tell you what you need.

I emphasize the word healthy in seeking outlets for working through grief because we can unknowingly add to our hurt. With my son dying in a work accident,

The Healing Journey

Michigan law required an autopsy and I was given a copy of the report. On the first two anniversaries of Robbie's death I reserved the day for mourning, which included the ritual of sitting down and reading the entire autopsy report. You may be wondering why I chose such a grisly and painful practice. Me too.

Before the third September 9th arrived, I realized what an unhealthy ritual I had concocted, and rather than drag myself through yet another round of self-inflicted torture, I decided to commemorate his birthday each year rather than the day he died. It felt so much better to affirm his life rather than his death and I haven't touched the autopsy report since.

Sometimes, when I'm driving, I see memorial markers people have erected to commemorate the spot where a loved one died. Though some may find this a comfort, it conflicts with my desire to affirm life, not death. I never went to the oil rig to see where my son died, figuring I just didn't need that picture in my head.

All Is Not Lost

But let me repeat that grief and healing are intensely personal. It's not a question of right and wrong, it's a question of finding our way to the point of accepting that things will never again be the same.

Picking up after a divorce brings its considerations, too. If children are involved, you and your ex will have to decide who gets the kids as the "firsts" unfold. You've probably seen other divorced couples jockeying for prime positions with vacations, holidays, birthdays, and other occasions.

After years of watching my daughter Cathy frantically juggling where she and Kris and the kids needed to be for the holidays, I suggested we celebrate our Christmas a week early; a healthy, workable choice we practice to this day.

Healing is about making choices that ease discomfort; little choices and big ones. Healing means choosing to believe that you will somehow find your way through the pain, even though some days it may not feel like it. It means having faith and knowing that even though you sometimes lose ground, you're still making progress, and that at some point the hurt will subside.

The hardest part about recovering from grief is having to accept that no matter how hard you try, or how many times you wish it, you cannot change the reality of what is. People (and pets) get sick or injured. Some die. Some of us get divorced or lose our jobs. Things happen. The more you resist the reality of what is, the worse you'll feel.

Persistently work your way toward accepting whatever element of reality represents your loss, because only by getting closer to the pain can you release it. As you progress through your struggles, periodically look back to note how far you've come. It's probably further than you thought.

All Is Not Lost

❦

A Healing Step

Following a death, divorce, or other life changing incident, special dates may cause some of your grief to spill over into other areas of your life. For your first one or two years especially, as those times roll around, you may find yourself crying or getting angry over trivial, unrelated issues; spilled coffee, a broken dish, misplacing your car keys. People around you may not realize what's going on because they've lost track. If it feels appropriate, let them know.

There will be days when it feels as if your emotions have taken on a life of their own, and in a way, they have. For the first year after a significant loss or change in your life, the wound is still tender and it will be a while before you're in full control of your emotions again. Don't get angry at yourself when you have a momentary breakdown. Accept it and be patient. Don't pretend your grief doesn't exist; let it work its way out.

The Healing Journey

Flashbacks and emotional rushes will occur, especially early on. Expect them. Let them run their course. In time they will diminish. Knowing that the "firsts" will be difficult after a death, resolve to handle them in a healthy manner. Create rituals that honor your loved one without being self-punishing. For the first decade after Robbie's death, Cathy would occasionally go to her brother's grave and talk to him. She says it made her feel better.

When your wound is still tender, you may temporarily hit the depths, and the key word is temporarily. If you find yourself feeling down for too long, that is, if your health, relationships, or work are affected, then seek professional help. There's no way around it, loss creates an empty space in your heart that takes a while to fill. But time will do its work if you allow it. Getting past the "firsts" is a series of critical steps in your healing journey. Take your time and take good care of yourself as you go.

All Is Not Lost

Chapter 7

SETBACKS AND IRONIES

There's no polite way to say it, sometimes you get hit when you're down. My friend Mary had to reckon with the death of both her parents within months of each other while another friend, Kathie lost not one, but two siblings in less than two years. Perhaps you, too, have had to cope with two or more crises within a disturbingly short period of time. Loss sometimes knows no bounds.

I think of my friend Mitchell who survived multiple broken bones and third degree burns over sixty percent of his body after the gas cap popped off his motorcycle when he was hit by a laundry truck. Miraculously, Mitchell survived his burns and went on with his life, becoming a successful business owner, the mayor of a small city, a congressional nominee, and certified pilot.

Mitchell's next challenge happened when the plane he was flying crashed. His passengers made it out safely but he didn't. This man who had already been through so much was left paralyzed by the accident. But even this setback didn't stop him.

Now an internationally recognized author and speaker, Mitchell lives the message found in his speeches as well as his book, *It's Not What Happens to You, It's What You Do With It.* This remarkable man survived two personal tragedies that would have stopped most people, but he kept on going. If you were to meet him you would be charmed by his charisma and touched by his wit and wisdom.

Setbacks can temporarily transport us back to square one, or at least that's how it feels, reminding us once again that while life is many things, fair is not one of them. We were only promised the pursuit of happiness, not happiness itself. While there's no way we can be fully prepared for hardships that may come, accepting the existence of loss or setbacks as a part of the life cycle is a good first step.

For me, Robbie's death was the first of three challenges I would face that fall. Two months after he died, Cathy's twin girls were born. My first grandchildren were a mixed blessing, as Cathy was unmarried and unemployed at the time.

Four weeks later, I had major surgery. These three life-altering events left me with little reserve, but my dear partner Rob was there for me, every minute of every day during those painful months. Even now, I appreciate his unconditional support because I don't know how I could have made it without him.

But everyone is not so fortunate. Sometimes, when tragedy strikes a family, everyone is so devastated it's impossible for them to reach out to one another. This is when a grief counselor or therapist is so critical.

The Healing Journey

That's where I would have gone had it not been for my supportive partner.

Five months after Robbie's death, I met a young woman exactly his age who had survived her recent suicide attempt. It felt eerie talking with someone who had wanted to die, but didn't. I couldn't help but think about my son, who didn't want to die, but did.

One of my clients, a small work team who suffered the suicide of a valued coworker, struggled to deal with their grief. Just as they had begun to make progress, a woman from a sister agency was killed in a domestic violence episode. Setbacks happen when we least expect them. And they hurt.

In a period of less than two years, my horse show pal Debby experienced more setbacks than some people will in a lifetime. Her saga began with having her car stolen and crashed by a supposedly trustworthy baby sitter, followed by the traumatic death of her favorite horse whose head Debby held in her arms while he breathed his last breath. As she recovered from this loss, her husband broke his neck, with the prognosis that his paralysis might be permanent. Within a few weeks of finding out that her mother's cancer had returned, Debby's brother died.

During a brief period of welcome diversion, Debby planned and hosted her best friend Sarah's wedding, but shortly afterward, Sarah was diagnosed with liver cancer. While she was given a life expectancy of several years, Sarah unexpectedly died within three weeks. A mere 100 days after the joyous wedding festivities, Debby found herself making all of the funeral arrangements and burying her dearest friend.

Debby's mother, who ended up in hospice care for over a year, welcomed her daughter's daily visits. During that year, Debby was summoned for last moments no less than six times and she was there to say goodbye when her mother died two weeks ago.

Despite her relentless setbacks, if you were to

meet Debby, the mother of three active, healthy children, a skilled rider, and horse owner once again, you would never guess this woman has withstood such adversity. Upbeat, bright, and witty, her philosophy is "count who's still there" and be grateful for what you have.

Debby says she keeps on going by counting on those who count on her, and that's exactly what she does. In case you're wondering, her husband has almost fully recovered from his injury.

Setbacks can be significant in scope and number, as in Debby's case, or a singular, seemingly small incident. When my ex mother-in-law died, her husband Joe was devastated. They had been married for nearly sixty years and it was hard for him to accept her being gone.

A few months after Ceil's death, as Joe sifted through her effects he found a card she had bought him for his birthday, signed, sealed, and tucked away. Finding it was almost more than he could bear.

When my friend Emory unexpectedly lost her husband, she mentioned several times how much it hurt, knowing that never again would she receive anything that bore George's wonderful, lush handwriting. The things we miss are sometimes odd and always intensely personal.

My clients who were struggling with the suicide of their coworker said their ears ached from listening for the sound of her wheel chair whizzing down the halls and into their offices. When Robbie died, my sons were living together and I will never forget Ron lamenting that even though his brother was gone, he could still smell his presence.

The survivors of September 11 have a longer, harder road than most of us. Some of them have endured not one, but months of funerals, strung along over time as the remains of loved ones were unearthed. Aside from their obvious loss and everyday hardships, they also have to cope, perhaps for years, with the long, complicated, convoluted procedure of receiving insurance, donations, and compensation for their lost loved ones due to the uniqueness of their circumstance.

Their healing journey is littered with heart breaking hurdles. Every time they stand in a line, make a phone call, keep an appointment, or fill out yet another form they relive some of their agony. Some will be dogged by the media or curiosity seekers.

Well over half of these survivors are women; many of them young wives and mothers, some of whom were pregnant when the tragedy occurred, giving birth to babies who will never know their fathers. These young women were forced to take on burdensome responsibilities they never dreamed of. I empathize with their recurring frustration, anger, and despair over what must feel like a living hell that will never go away.

All Is Not Lost

A Healing Step

If you are in the early stages of a crisis, it may seem that some days, just putting one foot in front of the other will be all you can do. Maybe it is. Yet, if you get knocked down, chances are you will somehow right yourself again, with the hope that tomorrow will be less difficult. Once you are able to accept that loss is as much a part of life as is happiness or success, you'll be better prepared to handle it.

Sadness and grief signal a time to go inward. If you want to heal you must go where you least want to, directly toward the hurt, so you can begin healing your heart and spirit. Learn about yourself, explore your feelings (all of them, the negative as well as the positive), and monitor what you're learning. This is where journaling can be helpful, as a means of not just expressing your emotions but for measuring your progress, too.

The Healing Journey

Every step along the way, help yourself accept what is, rather than wish for what isn't. If or when you meet up with a setback, stop and process what's going on. Grief is a stern teacher, but it presents us with lessons we can learn no other way. Although it may not seem like it right now while the hurt is still so fresh, there is a day when you will come out the other side of your hurt. Even if setbacks happen, miraculously, tediously, you will find the strength to get past them.

Simply put, a time of loss is a time to learn about yourself. Be as open and honest with yourself as you can. Your increased self-knowledge will make it easier to accept your vulnerability, conflicting feelings, and pain. You will become more comfortable with the discomforting reality that life comes with no guarantees. The more firm your faith, the easier it will be to access your inner strength to help you cope, recover, and sometimes even blossom, in spite of what happens to you.

All Is Not Lost

Chapter 8
GRIEVING 101

If you have buried a loved one, you know first hand the outrageous, stupid things people say to the grieving. More than one bereaving soul has reacted angrily to the well intentioned, "I know just how you feel." Because frankly, no they don't.

A man in one of my seminars told me he found little comfort in being told how happy he should feel because his son was now in heaven instead of with him. In the instance of a teen suicide, family members could not believe that so many people asked for all of the gory details.

I remember standing at my son's grave side while a woman I hadn't seen in years blithely prattled on about how well her family was doing, detailing each child's

The Healing Journey

accomplishments as I was burying one of mine. Maybe she hoped her verbalizing would somehow immunize her from a similar loss. Who knows. I was so numbed with grief I could barely listen anyway, but it did strike me as bizarre.

I suppose one could write a book about all of the things to not say while attempting to comfort someone in their time of loss. Grieving 101 maybe. Like me, you can probably come up with a long list of people who could use such a resource.

But given our culture's discomfort with grief, loss, and suffering, what can we expect? Some people feel so awkward, curious, uncomfortable, fearful, or embarrassed they don't say anything lest they say the wrong thing. But if they avoid us (and many do), we are left to interpret their disappearance in any number of ways. Do they feel bad for us? Do they wish there was something they could do? Do they not care? The possibilities are endless.

All Is Not Lost

Eight months after Robbie's death I received a note from a client who said she had put off contacting me because she felt terrible about my loss but could never find the right words to convey her sentiments. Finally, she decided to simply say she didn't know what to say, hoping that a late note of condolence was better than none at all. It was.

Generally speaking, people behave in ways that make sense to them, but their logic may completely escape the rest of us. So don't expect that people will always say or do what's appropriate; sometimes it's almost the opposite.

Now let's flip this picture. In your time of grief or crisis, people may have specific expectations about how you should be feeling and what you should be doing or not doing. Many will freely share their expectations, especially if you are not behaving as they think you should.

Six months after she lost her husband, Emory

decided to sell the secluded country home she and George had lived in, moving to town where she would feel less isolated. Some of her friends thought she was making a big mistake and they said so, but Emory knew this was right for her.

So we find that some friends say exactly what they think while others stay mum. When one of my friends divorced her husband following his affair, several of her acquaintances confided that this had been going on for years and they thought she knew. And although most people don't want to take sides, there are some, who following a separation, will tell you they thought you were nuts to have stayed with such a loser for so long. So much for honesty!

One of the hardest parts of a getting a divorce is that, if you have young children, things aren't really over. You will be exposed to your ex, even if you try to avoid him or her. If you remarry, or your ex does, then there's the issue of blended families, and if either of

All Is Not Lost

you decide to have another child, that can complicate your relationships with your existing children. Like it or not, those words from the marriage ceremony, "till death do us part" hold much significance.

Then there are the expectations people have about how long you should grieve. Regardless of the depth of your loss, some will get impatient with you, conveying an attitude of "get over it" even though they might not really say that.

Our time compressed culture allows for little grieving time. It's pretty much expected that within two or three weeks a person should be ready to bounce back after losing a loved one. A divorce? Well, you have the weekend to work on it. Not hardly.

My friend Segami told me that in ancient China mourning was not only allowed, but encouraged for 100 days. Compare that to our tolerance of less than a month. In remembering that the "firsts" are tough to deal with, I like to offer friends extended acknowledg-

ment the whole first year after they lose a loved one.
And I give similar attention to friends who are ill. My
expectation is that they can use it.

❦

A Healing Step

You already know this, but try to be tolerant
and forgiving of people's bizarre behaviors or inappro-
priate comments. In addition, save a generous amount
of patience and tolerance for yourself, too, because healing is a time consuming process.

Don't needlessly burden yourself with unrealis-
tic expectations about what you should be doing or not
doing, whether the expectations are your own, or those
of others. There is no prescription for grief.

Instead, listen to your body and mind. If you
need more healing time or just alone time, take it. If
you need to get away from someone who is asking taxing questions or making stupid comments, quietly ex-

cuse yourself and end the conversation. There is no formula or rule book that outlines how you must behave when you are in grief, but your inner wisdom will guide you through the process if you are willing to pay attention.

If you are newly divorced, you know it's in your best interest to find a civil way to communicate with your former partner. Too many couples keep their anger and bitterness alive and it can be traumatic for the kids. I find it ironic that, some couples, long since divorced, keep themselves inexorably bound up in a toxic relationship dedicated to perpetuating mutual misery.

That to me is the ultimate of living with loss. Think what they might have accomplished had they put that much energy into making their relationship work.

On the other hand, some ex spouses manage to be friends. These are the individuals who negotiate a successful separation, respecting their differences, and each other. How much better a way to live.

Whatever hardship you are facing, I hope there are people in your life who are there for you, friends or loved ones who will offer unconditional, long term support. And if someone you care about suffers a loss or illness, perhaps you can be there for them, maybe through that first 100 days, or even longer.

Our human nature makes us both imperfect and unpredictable. Sometimes you just don't know what's going to come out of someone's mouth (maybe even your own). Who knows, some of the bizarre remarks you hear may prompt a smile or even a laugh down the road when things aren't hurting quite so much.

All Is Not Lost

Chapter 9
HEALING RITUALS

When my son's life ended so suddenly, in addition to my shock and pain, I was angry that this young, healthy man with his whole life ahead of him was now dead. My ex-husband and his wife handled the funeral arrangements and for this I was grateful, but it also left a void.

With no immediate outlet for my anger, it took me only a few hours to realize that the minister who would bury my son had never met him and had no idea who he was. I found the idea of a stranger commenting on my son's life unacceptable. The night of Robbie's death I sat down and wrote his elegy.

After the funeral, people told me that the elegy which the minister so compassionately read gave them a vivid picture of my son and I took comfort in their comments. Though I was not yet a writer, this self-expression, born of anger, was a constructive way for me to vent my feelings.

But there was another step I needed to take, too. People seldom die when it's convenient and when Robbie died there was distance between us. Our unresolved issues hung heavily over me and the lack of closure was very hard to take.

If I could just go back in time, I would have immediately addressed our issues, but of course, this was impossible. Yet I knew I had to find a way to deal with my guilt and remorse. So I began writing a list of all the things I would have done differently if only I had known he was going to die, promising myself that this "If Only" list would be a one-time ritual.

For two weeks I added to my "If Only" list, crying and writing down every possible thought I could muster: If only I had initiated a conversation about our issues. If only I had told him how much I loved him. If only I had given him a real goodbye instead of a hurried one that last time I saw him. And so on. Racked with remorse, I diligently chronicled each of my regrets.

Once I felt I had exhausted my creativity, I stood alone in the back yard with my list. Sobbing, barely able to see through my tears, I read each "If Only" one last time. I then set a match to the pages of my pain. As my words turned into ash, I vowed that in releasing my regrets into the atmosphere, I would not revisit them. I've stuck to my promise. I certainly didn't know it at the time, but writing Robbie's elegy and creating a ritual that helped soothe the site of my sharpest pain had set my healing journey into motion.

Not all rituals need to be as serious as what I just described but they all function in the same way; to ease our discomfort and sense of loss. Three years ago one of my acquaintances sent a greeting card announcing her divorce and name change. It was humorous and quite festive, and for good reason. She had been in an oppressive relationship that had left her little room to grow. Breaking free, she felt herself opening up and blossoming like a languishing plant finally put in the light.

Another woman I know, as she felt herself beginning to heal from her hurt and pain after her husband of two decades left her for another woman, decided to create a slogan for herself: Betty's getting better all the time.

I have a copy of a newspaper article in my "inspiration" file of a woman I would love to meet. All her life, Linda Baker had dreamed of the day she'd walk down the aisle in a wedding gown, but at age forty she felt that time was running out and she had not yet found Mr. Right.

Instead of grieving over her lost dream she decided to marry herself and become Mrs. Right. There's a photo accompanying the article showing her in a lovely full length gown, feeding herself a piece of wedding cake. She is a wonderful example of facing what could be a serious disappointment with lightness and wit.

It truly is a case of whatever works. After the painful ending of her long term relationship, my friend Marta rearranged her home over a period of time, shifting entire rooms around, altering her living space as recognition that her life had undergone a drastic change.

One of my friends asked me to write her a special poem for her fiftieth birthday. Oddly enough (or maybe not) the way I began the poem was exactly what Barbara had already planned for herself the morning of her birthday.

I encourage you to plan and hold whatever ritual will help you commemorate a passage in your life. It could involve healing a deep hurt, letting go of, or welcoming a new era. There was a time after my divorce when I was on welfare, attending community college, raising my kids, and trying to make something of myself. It was a challenging, scary, and exciting period.

The Healing Journey

When I received my associate degree and found a job that would actually sustain my kids and me (unlike my first job) I was jubilant. To celebrate this achievement I handmade some cards and sent them to friends announcing that I was now getting off welfare, going back to work, and "reentering society."

Many years later, rather than dread turning the big "Five Oh" I celebrated turning fifty the entire year, keeping fresh flowers in my home at all times and shamelessly announcing my passage to almost anyone who would listen. I am doing the same as I approach my sixtieth birthday. You get the point. Closure, resolution, and marking a passage are key elements in the process of moving on.

A Healing Step

Rituals can ease your feelings of loss. Keep in mind that all rituals don't all have to be serious or solemn. Some people face life with flair and whimsy, even when they hurt. If you are in transition or are struggling with regret, anger, or a difficult issue, consider a healing ritual. You could write out your feelings in a poem, a letter of apology, regret, goodbye, appreciation, or anger; whatever you need to get off your chest.

If you are embarking on a new chapter in your life, you could write your own declaration of independence. A divorce liberation ritual could help you focus on your new life instead of the old one. You could purify your home by burning sage, having it blessed, or creating a candlelight ceremony with your best friends bearing witness to your social passage.

You could create your own "If Only" list. You could write a letter to yourself, pretending to be the person who has caused you pain that explains why he or she behaved this way. I've used this ritual when I have been betrayed because it gives me a chance to view things from the other person's perspective.

The Healing Journey

As you can see, rituals and cleansing exercises are very personal. Some are meant to be private, some are public, and some of what you commit to paper is not meant to be kept. Using fire as I did to burn a document isn't necessary, but I am drawn to fire because it's so primal and offers a sense of finality. If open flames aren't an option because of your living circumstances you could tear your document into a thousand pieces, dropping them one by one into a special bag or container that you could bury or dispose of in whatever way you see fit.

Whether your ritual takes the form of writing, listening to a piece of music, reciting a prayer or a poem, dancing or acting out your grief, or holding some kind of ceremony, the important part is that it represents a step in the process of letting go and moving on. We have so few rituals and rites of passage in our culture, I encourage you to consider what kind of observance might soothe your hurt so you can move along.

All Is Not Lost

Chapter 10
GETTING IT

We all know we are mortal creatures and we've been reminded a thousand times that life is not a dress rehearsal, yet it's still hard to contemplate our own demise. As I watch the perpetually hurried masses recklessly speeding on the road, more preoccupied with their careers and investment portfolio than their relationships or personal safety, I wonder if they really get it that one day they will die.

Some of us got it for a while after September 11. Not just at ground zero but all across our country, I saw people behaving differently. Strangers waved at each other, people were more polite in stores or while waiting in lines, and drivers even slowed down. This period of enlightenment lasted about two months. By

The Healing Journey

Thanksgiving, many people were back to being impatient, rushed, and rude again. Speeding and tailgating returned to the road. We seemed to have forgotten about death and destruction as we returned to business as usual, full speed ahead.

Life has been jokingly described as a terminal condition that takes no survivors. Still, we're shocked when someone dies. I still remember my surprise when the oncologist confirmed that dad's cancer was terminal. At this writing he is still alive, and watching my father handle his illness has been a real education, mostly mine.

Early on, I got frustrated with dad because he didn't want to learn about his illness, nor would he read, listen to tapes, meditate, or try any self-treatment that might make him more comfortable. I impatiently waited for him to get it; that this was his body and his illness and he needed to take charge. But finally, I was the one who got it. I was expecting my father to face his illness

my way, not his way. This taught me that sometimes we
have more to let go of than grief.

Thanks to the combination of age and experience, I've come to fully appreciate the fleeting nature of
life and the precious nature of enduring relationships.
In the past two years alone, three friends of mine have
lost their spouses. I have lost two acquaintances to cancer, people who had to hear the dreaded words, "You
are going to die." But then, we all are, aren't we.

Maybe we each need to pay our doctors to sit
us down and look us in the eye and say, "You are going
to die. Get it?" Because those words apply to every one
of us. The only part we don't know is when. What a
difference it makes, not knowing when.

A Healing Step

If you are reading this book it's probably because you're experiencing some kind of loss, or antici-

pating one. You've probably already reckoned with the cold idea of knowing things don't last forever. People die, marriages end, accidents happen, some of us get sick, some of us get well, and some of us don't.

As you emerge from your current challenge and begin putting the pieces of your life back together, think about how what you've been through will cause you to live differently. Maybe you've already made a mental list of what truly matters and you have told the special people in your life how important they are. I hope so.

Crisis, grief, and loss are really about change, and some of these changes hurt. Avoidance is a poor option because there's no way you can sidestep the pain or the change. But if you resist too much you could miss the lessons that accompany the hurt.

Perhaps what you've experienced will help you slow down, pay more attention, savor your moments of joy, or more openly demonstrate your affection. I can't count the number of times my parents and I have said

All Is Not Lost

"I love you," to each other since dad was diagnosed. But I could count the times before then. Dad's illness significantly changed us.

Sometimes crisis is the only way we get the lesson of not taking things for granted. September 11 was a massive wake up call that inspired some individuals to go through the rest of their days with a new clarity about what life is and isn't. Death and loss have many lessons to teach us about living if we are willing to work through our hurt.

There are those of us who live with the sober awareness that you just don't know what will happen tomorrow and accepting the reality of impermanence and uncertainty affects how we live. Then there are those who refuse to think about any of this at all. Which, in your mind, represents the biggest loss?

The Healing Journey

Chapter II

THE STOCKPILE OF SORROW

Crisis brings with it a rush of mixed emotions, often more than we might expect, as unresolved losses and pain from the past join up and merge with our present. When you face a period of grief, old wounds or regrets may coalesce, unleashing a flood of unresolved hurt. If you are not aware of this "stockpile of sorrow" you may be taken off guard by the emotional upwelling.

Any significant loss can dredge up every previous hurt, mistake, or fiasco we ever had a hand in, dating back to childhood. The trauma of losing a job, for example, can resurrect past feelings of failure, shame, and inadequacy. Like death and illness, job loss connects to our sense of survival. When we lose our job we

All Is Not Lost

lose a little part of ourselves.

Our first reaction is usually a rush of fear over what will happen to us, followed by anger at the unfairness of it all. As our confidence erodes, old feelings of not being good enough resurface. Regardless of what we may have accomplished in our life, job loss, demotion, or a career downgrade can temporarily make us feel as if we still don't measure up.

Then there's divorce. The end of a significant relationship can release a wash of guilt, regret, insecurity and more, in addition to anger or disappointment. Even if we know that divorce is the best option we may still be haunted by second guessing and a sense that maybe there was more we could have, or should have done. The regret we feel over the end of a marriage can unearth guilt, self-doubt, and inadequacy from other relationships we weren't able to hold together.

Of course, our feelings of letdown, hurt, and self-recrimination are magnified if the reason we're divorcing centers around a betrayal. Regardless of how well adjusted any of us may be, we all seem to carry our own issues of abandonment and rejection, and it hurts. If this is your case, rather than focusing on the rejection and letting it erode your self-esteem, remind yourself that your partner's behavior says more about him or her than it does about you.

When I got divorced my three kids were well under ten years old. Knowing that this change was traumatic for them too, I tried to appear as calm as I could and give them a sense of stability. Inside, I was terrified. I had no job skills and seriously doubted if I could make it on my own. I had never worked, except to clean people's houses or do their baskets of ironing.

Pitifully lacking in work skills and self-confidence, I knew I had to set the tone for my children. It took everything I had to appear confident, because the end of my marriage marked yet another dismal failure in a lifelong succession of personal fiascoes.

All Is Not Lost

Not only was I panicked at the prospect of being on my own, I was also filled with shame. Having been such a troublesome child and rebellious teen, I was never popular. I had flunked algebra in the ninth grade and dropped out of school not once, but twice. I was pregnant when I got married, and now I was a failure as a wife. The stockpile of insecurities and fears from my past nearly immobilized me. Small wonder I was so angry and defensive the first few years after my divorce; I was carrying a huge load of mental baggage.

Not one to learn all of life's lessons in a flash, I gave myself more opportunities to revisit my psychological stockpile when I was almost fired from my first two jobs. After being forced through not one, but two such moments of reckoning, I began to realize that while I did have some potential, I had kept it cleverly hidden all those years. It was time to trade my denial and defensiveness for responsibility. Finally, I came to terms with my past, and from there I began slowly, systematically setting my sites on a new, more positive future.

But once in awhile, even as far as I've come in my life, when I feel I've made a huge mistake, I can feel some of my old inadequacies resurfacing. These days I have enough confidence to keep things in perspective and not let myself get too overwhelmed with old issues, but it took time and persistent effort to neutralize my sketchy past.

❦

A Healing Step

The point is that we all have our issues and until we come to terms with them, they can gang up on us in a crisis. Remind yourself that losses which appear quite straightforward are often threaded to a complex strand of companion issues begging to be reckoned with and that's why a crisis can feel so complicated. Resolve your issues now and get them behind you, because if you don't, they'll simply pile up and come back to haunt

All Is Not Lost

you when you are your most vulnerable.

Earlier in this book I mentioned that grieving is a private, personal time; a time meant for you to go inside and sort through the hurt you feel. If you try to avoid your inner work by losing yourself in busyness and distraction, the unresolved pain will patiently lurk in the shadows until a quiet moment when your guard is down.

Once again, if you don't give yourself time to sort through these issues, much of what you feel will get stockpiled, coming back to torment you at a later date.

During times of loss, treat yourself as kindly as you would a cherished friend. This may sound like a cliche, but if you take care of the healing process it will take care of you. It doesn't feel like it right now, but life is out there, waiting for you.

Healing will happen. How else could it be that so many people once traumatized by a divorce, the loss of a job, and even health emergencies exclaim, "It was the best thing that ever happened to me!" Of course, this is not always the case, but even the worst of our experiences can teach worthy lessons about how to live, and maybe even die.

If just the thought of bereavement, grief, or crisis seems depressing, remind yourself that there is something even more depressing. Think of the countless people who refuse to do their inner work because they're afraid of what they'll find. They keep trying to close a door that has no latch.

These unfortunate individuals will spend their entire lives in a long term, low level state of denial and grief. The stockpile of sorrow they unknowingly carry prevents them from fully experiencing clarity, fulfillment, and joy. They're hampered by the mire of past hurts they refuse to let go of. Don't let that happen to you.

All Is Not Lost

Chapter 12
GOODBYE CAN MEAN GOODBYE

We have rules in our household about saying goodbye. The basic requirements include eye contact and face to face acknowledgment. We tolerate no automatic, empty gestures, no yelling from the door, no turned backs, and no air kisses that fall to the floor, orphaned, unrequited. When we say goodbye, even when running out for a quick errand, we make it an event.

In fact, Rob and I have made a game of saying goodbye. One of us will stand at the door, announcing our departure, hesitating long enough for the other to come running from another room in mock frenzy, ready to dispense a farewell hug or kiss.

You may be wondering if we've always had this rule. Of course not. Following my son's death I was haunted by the distant, preoccupied farewell I had given him. I have no recollection of whether I kissed or hugged him or looked into his eyes. I suspect I did not. My brain was already on the road, eager to get home and back to my routine. After having to own up to my negligence that day, I vowed to never again to be so arrogant. This was a harsh, painful lesson.

Given my history, you can imagine the empathy I felt for those who lost loved ones on September 11. My heart ached for the hundreds, perhaps thousands of people who gave their own incomplete goodbyes that fateful morning. Some were still asleep when their partners walked out the door. A few left in anger. How could anyone have dreamed that this casual, everyday gesture would take on such significance a few hours later?

For those of us whose last goodbye left so painfully much unsaid, we must come to accept that this was only one moment and not the whole relationship. It is a deed that cannot be undone and there's a point at which we need to give up flogging ourselves for our inability to predict the future. As far as the future goes, we can only pledge to make each of our goodbyes something to remember.

❧

A Healing Step

Maybe you already give great goodbyes, but if not, I encourage you make each one an event, even if it's only your pet you are leaving behind. If like me, you live with a remorseful goodbye, remind yourself that it was only a moment in time and you do not possess psychic powers. Forgive yourself.

We can serve ourself and the memory of our loved one by focusing on the meaningful hours and days and years when we were intimately connected instead of the brief moments we were not. We cannot change our history, but our past has worthwhile lessons to teach us as we move on.

The Healing Journey

Some people wrap themselves in their pain instead of learning from it. Don't fall into that trap. We all have regrets and our job is to put them in perspective and learn what they can teach us. Regret can turn us toward what we truly value. Grief can remind us how precious life is. Disappointment can help us clarify what we want. Mistakes can provide us with the opportunity to try something different, to create new patterns and practices that enrich our existence.

Who would think that a simple goodbye, one of the first social gestures we learn as babies, and one we so casually engage in without a thought countless times a day, could hold such consequence.

All Is Not Lost

Chapter 13

HEALING MIND, HEALING BODY

If you've ever seriously pulled a muscle, broken a bone, or had surgery, your recovery period probably took longer than you wanted it to. At first you were probably content to take it easy but later on you got restless because getting better was taking way too long. If you got impatient and pushed yourself you may have paid for it by reinjuring the wound.

Well, healing from an emotional injury follows the same slow course as physical healing, only it takes even longer because there are often circumstances that prolong the process. For one, you've probably found yourself explaining your new situation over and over again, as you run into people who have no idea what's happened.

The Healing Journey

The combination of repeating your experience and watching the shock or dismay on people's faces can refresh some of your hurt. So can everyday incidents such as receiving mail addressed to your deceased loved one (or ex), taking his or her phone calls from acquaintances who don't yet know, or telemarketers who don't care.

Because inner wounds cannot be seen, it's hard to comprehend how intricately they connect to our physical being. But talk with anyone who has had body-work (for example, deep tissue massage such as Rolfing and Hellerwork; Reiki or craniosacral therapy) and they will tell you how buried emotional pain can be connected to chronic physical distress. If you suffer a recurring infirmity or physical discomfort, you might try some bodywork. It certainly has helped me.

If you doubt that an unresolved emotional injury can manifest itself physically, think of the Post Traumatic Stress Disorder that has plagued thousands of Viet Nam veterans for decades now. It would not surprise me if we were to witness an upsurge of low level depression, anger outbursts, and vague physical ailments in our population for months and even years to come as a result of unresolved personal traumas spawned by September 11. Maybe it will even get its own name.

Understanding the connection between the mind and body brings us to the issue of how we might be able to prevent a trauma from taking root in our physical self. The day of Robbie's funeral, I woke up in more pain than I've ever felt in my life and I've gone through childbirth three times, have had horses bite and kick me, toss me off, even fall on me. I've had surgery, minor accidents, and more invasive dental work and medical procedures than I'd like to own up to, but I had never felt anything like this.

My mind ached. My body felt as if I had been beaten and my spirit throbbed with pain. My first waking thought was, "I just want to die, too." But my thoughts didn't end there. Immediately, the phrase, "I can make it through this day," filled my mind. In spite of my agony, those words helped me get up that awful morning.

"I can make it through this day," became my mantra for that agonizing day and the ones that followed. Later, I realized, with gratitude, that my years of practicing self-encouragement had become as much a part of me as breathing. The mental discipline of thinking rationally and repeating affirmations to bolster myself when facing threatening situations had indeed become a habit, preparing me for the hardest moments of my life.

I'm suggesting that words influence our perceptions and our perceptions influence our behavior, and while there exists a multitude of examples, let's focus on one: our everyday exposure to ads, product names, or store displays. When words and images are put together powerfully, both our mind and body connect with the message. We have a visceral reaction, which often means we end up buying something we hadn't planned on purchasing.

Start paying attention to how words affect your perceptions and behavior, not only in a commercial context, but everyday interactions, too. Because language not only shapes the way we see our world, but influences us at a physical level, I encourage you to be more conscious of what you think about. The words you use will either influence the depth of your pain or the breadth of your healing; it's your choice. You can use encouraging language to help you heal after a divorce or job loss. You can make deliberate decisions about how you want to remember a lost loved one.

I loved my son's irreverent sense of humor. My favorite memory of him is when he met a dog that was missing its right front leg. As a puppy, CJ had been hit by a car and although he received immediate medical attention, CJ's leg could not be saved. As Robbie looked at this canine "tripod," he turned to Carol, the dog's owner, and asked wryly, "Can he shake?" Telling this story, especially in the early days of my bereavement, helped ease both my mental and physical hurt.

In times of hardship, consciously monitor what you're thinking. When one of my newly divorced acquaintances was in the early stages of grief, she talked about how hard it was sifting through what she called emotional "ick." I winced at the word. It not only told me that she was hurting, but she had inadvertently chosen to view the work she needed to do as undesirable.

Though I am not the first to line up when a sign announces "Get your free pain here!" I know there's something in it for me if I'm willing to root around in those sensitive places. Let me explain.

All gardeners know that a good fertilizer enriches an otherwise languishing soil bed. We could call the primary ingredient in fertilizer "ick," but think of what it does. Fertilizers provide essential nutrients for the soil, making it a more nourishing environment for the plants we want to thrive and blossom. I am suggesting that what my friend called "ick" is a similar nutrient for the mind and soul. It's a messy process, to be sure, but deep in the "ick" lie insights and revelations that help us heal and grow. I even have a name for it: emotional pay dirt.

Because of the word she's using, this woman may be reluctant to stick around as long as it takes to root through the "ick" and find the insights and comfort that await her. In the long run, this could end up compounding her loss because unresolved hurt may well manifest itself in physical symptoms later on and she won't have a clue.

A Healing Step

I can't possibly know what mental wounds you

are currently dealing with, but you do. Regardless of your crisis, once the shock and disbelief begin subsiding, you can minimize some of the pain and help your mind and body heal by consciously choosing what you think about.

Instead of getting swept away in despair, repeat a special affirmation whenever you feel the need, saying something like, "When I think about _____ I will focus on _____." I'm suggesting you choose a positive aspect instead of focusing on how much you hurt. A favorite memory of someone who has died can help you smile through your tears and provide a welcome wave of relief for your mind and body.

Focusing on your commitment to recover from a crushing betrayal can summon strength you didn't know you had. This approach can also be applied in combating illness or fear. Like any other skill, affirmations require practice. If you've never done anything like this before, in the beginning it can feel awk-

All Is Not Lost

ward, silly, and ineffective.

It's hard attempting something strange and new when you feel down, but give it a try anyway. Just a bit of self-encouragement can bring comfort. If, at the moment, you are not in a state of crisis there's no better time to begin your practice so these skills will be there, if, or when you need them in the future.

Healing requires a blend of the familiar and the unfamiliar. Of course, you'll want to read and re-read the sources that best reflect your faith or spiritual practice, yet there's no better time than now to try something you've never done before. Consider doing some bodywork, seeing a therapist, or maybe even consulting a healer. Try anything else that appeals to you.

I know a woman who says that sometimes seeing her psychic is as effective as seeing her psychologist. One of my friends, Mary Jane, would immediately turn to scripture in times of crisis while my pal Sparky would break out the Tarot deck or consult her numerologist.

The Healing Journey

Again, it's an issue of whatever works for you. One thing is clear. Your life has changed. This makes it a fitting time to explore options that lie outside of your comfort zone because, well, you're already there anyway.

Pain is a natural, normal part of life but it is not a "normal" state. Granted, there are those unfortunate individuals whose illnesses or injuries have rendered them in a state of chronic pain and they have my deepest sympathy. For the rest of us, pain is a signal that something needs to be addressed.

When you suffer a loss, it may feel at first as if you'll never get beyond the hurt, but you will. For a while, healing is a full time job. Many people try to avoid the work, not realizing that by denying their pain and trying to escape from it, they short circuit the healing process, keeping their wounds fresh and tender. They don't realize that acceptance is the restorative tonic that gradually and gently heals not only the mind, but the body, too.

All Is Not Lost

Your toughest experiences stand to teach you the most about not only who you are, but who you are becoming. Take mental notes, encourage yourself and be patient. The process will probably take longer than you like, or think it should take, but stay with it. In time your mind and body will heal and you will rediscover life's joys.

Chapter 14
LETTING GO

People often say it's easier to remember the sad times than the happy ones. Maybe we're more inclined to remember the painful times because they seem more vivid. For example, the phrase "I love you," is usually delivered softly and gently, but "I hate you," comes out with force and volume. I'm not suggesting that we should shout our love but it's clear which of these messages will more likely stick.

A few years ago, scientists discovered that one of the reasons we remember traumatic events is because of the presence of adrenaline in our system. Adrenaline raises our sense of keenness and sensitivity. It helps us take an "emotional snapshot" of the incident, etching it into our memory bank.

And then there's the very human characteristic of mental replay, a self-defeating practice most of us naturally excel in. Just like rewinding and replaying a video tape, our brain can replay hurtful memories with remarkable detail, and with every repetition we feel the pain all over again.

If you've been hurt, disappointed, or betrayed, you've probably spent considerable time thinking about it. Maybe you muddled over how the situation could have been prevented or better handled. Maybe you ran a few hundred alternate scenarios, things that never ac-

All Is Not Lost

tually happened, but could have. I must confess, I've done all of this.

Oddly enough, the hurt we feel every time we go through a replay doesn't stop us. We keep at it, as if running through the footage one more time could somehow change the past. Yes, this is rather bizarre behavior when you really look at it, and it's also a vivid example of how hard it is letting go. I have known people who suspended themselves in a state of grieving for so long that this became the only way they knew how to live.

Others remain bitter over something that happened decades ago, blaming that single, pivotal event for anything that goes wrong in their lives. It's sad that some individuals stubbornly, obstinately hold onto old pain as if they would be lost without it. These poor people haven't learned how to let go.

Maybe it would help if we all understood that by its nature, grief is meant to be a temporary state and that's why it's so intense. The person who chooses to

The Healing Journey

replay a painful experience doesn't realize that once the incident has passed, the hurt that lingers is mostly self-imposed. They don't realize that they're stuck in a self-perpetuating loop of their own creativity and persistence.

I'll be the first to admit letting go is difficult, but it's not impossible. In my life, on two different occasions, I have heard first hand accounts of horrors that happened during the Holocaust. In hearing what these survivors had witnessed, I couldn't fathom that any human beings, particularly children, could have survived such terror without becoming psychotic. Talk about the healing spirit!

While each story was different, there was a striking similarity in the outcome. Both of these stalwart souls accepted their traumatic history and each went on to establish a life that offered meaning and fulfillment. If they could let go, so can the rest of us.

All Is Not Lost

A Healing Step

If you've been victimizing yourself with repeated painful flashbacks, stop. In other words, refuse to get swept away in your pain. Remind yourself that no matter how many times you hit "replay," the past is unchangeable. You can't control or remake the past, but you surely can hurt yourself with it.

I encourage you to let go of your old mental tape and replace it with a new version. In other words, consciously think about something in the present or recall a memory that warms your heart. Repetition is the key. Keep repeating the new thought track until it overtakes the old. This is how world class athletes improve their performance and I encourage you to perfect this powerful skill to help you prevail over adversity. Remember, you control what you think about right now, and that influences your future.

Only by letting go of your past hurts or injustices can you move forward. It is self-defeating to keep insisting that life is not fair or that bad things shouldn't happen. Bad things happen to all of us. Life brings both the good and the bad; and we can move on anyway.

In the case of healing from the death of a loved one, remember that you honor him or her by continuing to live as fully as possible. Let the healing progress through its natural stages; sort out the pieces, slowly repair what hurts, and let yourself return to the business of living. By mourning a death for too long, you deprive those who are still alive your much needed attention and affection.

The same principle applies to a painful divorce. At some point you need to let go of your anger or regret, and positively direct that energy toward yourself or your children who need your attention and comfort. We are mobile creatures, meant to move. Ask yourself what you need to let go of so you can move on. John Gray's *Mars and Venus Starting Over* offers some insights about the stages you may go through.

If you feel you need help with any part of this process and don't have a friend or intimate loved one you can be open with, then find a support group or skilled therapist. I fully agree with the statement "where there's life, there's hope." Hope is the fuel that keeps us moving forward in spite of our hurt.

Chapter 15
OTHER LOSSES

Change is a constant in life and it is often accompanied by some kind of loss. Even our circle of friends changes with the years: we leave some of them behind and some of them leave us. When my best friend Roxanne moved to Seattle I didn't realize it meant the end of our friendship and I grieved the loss for years.

The Healing Journey

Having seen her a few times since then, I've come to realize that the woman I so sorely missed no longer exists. We have little in common now.

Work represents its own set of losses, large and small. Job loss shakes the foundation of our existence because it jeopardizes our entire way of living. Considering the number of hours spent in the workplace and the uncontrollable issues that go along with it (conflicting agendas and personalities, time demands, politics, ego clashes, unresponsive or incompetent management, to name a few) it's no surprise that work can represent an ongoing source of distress.

Job changes such as reorganizations, reassignments, and reclassifications can mean losing our connections with former peers who now perceive us differently or shy away because we are no longer a part of the old team.

Promotions often bring with them unexpected burdens such as increased responsibilities, longer hours, and people problems. With demotions, the loss of status can be ego crushing. Clearly, the workplace can be the source of many losses.

One person's trauma can be invisible to others. There are people who grieve the loss of natural habitat just as others would mourn a lost loved one, taking the constant damage to our environment very personally. Edward Abbey, author of the evocative *Desert Solitaire*, is one example. His subsequent works vibrated with anger as he watched so many cherished wild places destroyed.

One of my favorite authors, Carl Hiaasen, chronicles similar insults in his Miami Herald column. I respect how he has sublimated his grief over the systematic destruction of his home state's shorelines and ecology by writing novels that pulsate with vicious, brilliant humor and evil characters. Hiaasen is an example of how you can creatively channel your indignation or angst instead of ruining your health (or life) over circumstances that lie outside of your control.

Earlier in the book I discussed the losses that accompany aging, though getting older has become a different issue than it was a few decades ago. Just look around at the emerging seniors (like myself). Old is younger than it used to be, and with an assist from medical technology, we can even turn back the odometer: many of my professional speaker colleagues are postponing the loss of their youth with various forms of cometic surgery. This is an option I have not exercised, nor do I plan to.

But mind you, I qualify. I don't even officially fit into "middle age" anymore. Perhaps I'm clinging to a thin strand of denial, but there are moments this still takes me by surprise. So far, thanks to regular exercise, my mother's genes, and moderately healthy diet I'm in pretty good shape, with only a few isolated parts of my body knowing how old I really am.

I did give up jogging some years ago to relieve

the wear and tear on my knees. Otherwise, I'm still actively learning, thinking creatively, riding my horse, hiking, and coming pretty close to doing to what I've always done. For this, I am mightily grateful.

🌿

A Healing Step

Even small losses or changes can prompt unease. If you find yourself feeling down or angry, take time to pinpoint where it's coming from or what it's connected to, especially if you have experienced any recent changes. Was there an expectation that didn't get met? Have you been ignoring any physical symptoms? Have you been avoiding an issue you need to deal with? Check the calendar. A pending birthday, especially one that moves you into a new decade, or other significant dates can trigger feelings and thoughts you didn't know you had. Old anniversaries, even long after a death or divorce can resurface old wounds or regrets.

The Healing Journey

Maybe there's something you're grieving over and you've resisted admitting it. You might have tried to convince yourself that you're being silly or stupid, but feelings are feelings and they will let themselves be known one way or the other.

We've discussed how personal a loss can be. We've also established that if you don't address the emotions that are trying to come out, they'll express themselves later somewhere in your body. Be efficient. It's like our moms used to tell us when we were neglecting our chores: go "inside" and get your work done now, so that if anything comes along that you want to do, you'll be free to do it.

All Is Not Lost

Chapter 16
LIFE AND DEATH IN HAPPY LAND

In our culture we take extreme measures to isolate ourselves from death, illness, disability; the side of life that makes us queasy or uncomfortable. I remember a colleague of mine, an intelligent woman, stating that she had decided to just skip menopause because it didn't sound like any fun. She meant it.

Though life presents us with different forms of loss, disappointment, or sadness from childhood on, we're not encouraged to dwell on them. Maybe as a child, you remember being dissuaded from showing your hurt. With the best of intentions, parents often tell a sad child to not feel that way; to smile or be happy instead. Even in today's gender sensitive world, when boys cry they may be told to stop, or even "That didn't hurt!"

The Healing Journey

We learn to deny our feelings at an early age.

The message most of us end up with is that basically it's good to be happy and bad to be blue. We see thousands of commercials encouraging us to buy products that are supposed to make us feel good, from cosmetics and hygiene products to over the counter medications and prescription drugs.

We have so many diversions and social conventions shielding us from reality that we can pretty much pretend the untidy, less glamorous aspects of living and dying don't even exist. Small wonder some of us go off the deep end when eventually forced to face serious loss or grief first hand. We're such raw rookies.

Psychologists say it is human nature to embrace pleasure and avoid pain. This makes sense at first blush, and yet some of my most transforming moments have been connected in some way to a period of growth (read pain) and personal change. I think of the times Rob and I worked so hard on our relationship, weeks and months on end, because we were at the point where it was either split up or work it out. Difficult, yes, but these were also some of the most intimate, passionate periods of my life.

We talked, cried, talked some more, and made love as if it might be our last. Talking things out was gut wrenching work, and I wouldn't have missed it for the world. The results were life changing, for both of us. We're still together and still crazy about each other. Like best friends, only better.

At the risk of sounding immodest I would say that Rob and I have been courageous in the management of our relationship. Yes, we've made mistakes. Lots of them. And we've been willing to own up and work through our respective issues. As a couple we've had the fortitude to venture toward the raw, uncomfortable edge of existence where insight dwells, gaining wisdom we could have gotten no other way.

Most of us are not taught to work on our relationships, or our lives, for that matter. In trying to address conflicts or broach tough subjects with our partners, we may be told to not rock the boat, or that we think too much. In my marriage, when I wanted to talk about issues, my husband would put his hand up defensively and say, "Don't get into my head!"

It's uncomfortable talking about problems but in the long run it's even more uncomfortable avoiding them. Maybe if more of us were to choose the short term discomfort of conflict resolution for the sake of long term gain we could save a few relationships and hack down the divorce rate.

But we're not encouraged to fight for our relationships and few of us know how. No one tells us it's our right or maybe even our duty to willfully go right up to, and maybe a little past the edge of emotional discomfort to learn, grow, or save our bond. We'd rather believe the commercials and music and fairy tales that tell us all you need is love plus a few of the right products, and you'll get everything you want, including a romance that leads to the land of happily ever after.

And while we are spoon fed the fantasy of how good life should be, we get the impression that death is sad, ugly, painful, undignified, and messy. These are not things we like in our society. So we shun the untidy issues of illness, death, and aging until they are impossible to avoid.

A Healing Step

While we often expect death to be sad, ugly, painful, undignified, and messy, it can also be peaceful, tender, intimate, inspiring, and transcendent. The quality of the experience depends a good deal on the circumstances surrounding the death, who we are going into the experience, and the extent to which we accept our situation.

Knowing who you are and being comfortable

with who you are will help you handle the isolation and loneliness of facing hardship and loss. If you were to review your most enlightening moments, you'd find that your revelations came from the tough periods when you were forced to own up or discover new aspects of yourself. This is what I mean by going up to the edge of pain. That's where the richest lessons are.

Loss, grief, or crisis provide you with opportunities to honestly explore your feelings and beliefs because for a limited time, you will see things differently. The same painful experience that sets you apart from others also provides a special vantage point for viewing your existence. As you begin to heal, this keen vision will slowly disappear, so pay attention to what you observe during this period.

As a matter of course, when you learn about life, you learn about death or loss, and vice versa. Once you accept these connections, the preciousness of your own existence and how you want to live becomes clearer.

All Is Not Lost

Chapter 17

EARLY LOSSES, LATER LEARNING

As children we are curious, naive, open, innocent, ready to learn, and filled with trust; more on our own than it may appear, we have a thousand questions but few people to answer them. We feel powerless in a world run by adults or older siblings; everyone is in control but us.

In looking back on your childhood you might find more loss than you expect. Somewhere in your childhood, perhaps your trust was betrayed. Maybe you were sexually abused, bullied by your older siblings, punished unfairly, too harshly, or too often, or outright neglected by adults who had trouble coping with the stresses and responsibilities of parenthood.

When you were a child you probably had a

moment when you vowed, "When I grow up, I'll never (spank, yell at, embarrass, swear at, lie to, or belittle) my children as my parents did!" But perhaps to your dismay, you have heard your parent's words coming out of your own mouth. I certainly have.

Early traumas can leave marks that don't surface till adulthood, where behavior patterns end up being repeated though generations. In other words, the physically abused child can become the abuser as an adult. The child who grew up in a alcoholic home may become one, or marry one. Though it doesn't always happen, psychologists state that these and less extreme patterns are likely to be repeated over and over again, unless an individual comes to terms with early losses.

The point is that you don't have to hurt all your life, and you don't have to take your past out on others. This is especially important if you have children. If you are part of an unhealthy, repetitious cycle you can break it. Do it on your own, or with the help of a professional. But do it.

Maybe you are one of the fortunate individuals whose history was less extreme and your early losses didn't include outright abuse or neglect. That pretty much describes my childhood, but I still had many losses, times of intense confusion, and angst.

I was terribly sensitive, but tried to cover it up with toughness. Between my insatiable curiosity and my nonstop mouth I could get into trouble without trying, and I did. My dad's mother had a rug in her living room that I adored. Woven with deep, rich colors, the rug depicted two dogs sitting side by side, as old friends might. I loved it. One day I asked, "Grandma, when you kick the bucket can I have this rug?" Our relationship was never the same.

My best friend turned first boy friend, Victor Banks, moved to Colorado when I was five years old. I missed him for a surprisingly long time. I had thought we would grow up and get married one day but then he left and was out of my life forever. This was my first grieving experience. Even as an adult I found myself wondering what happened to Victor and the first time I visited Denver I looked for his name in the phone book.

No one ever knew how I felt about losing Victor but if they had, it would have been labeled "puppy love" and they would have said I'd get over it. But I didn't for a long time. In telling this story I realized that, unless we're dealing with death or divorce, we tend to trivialize a child's grief.

I idolized my kindergarten and first grade teacher, Miss McNally, and hated having to move into the stern Mrs. Sandeen's second grade. I took comfort in knowing I would progress to a new reading level, but I secretly mourned losing my connection with Miss McNally.

One December day Mrs. Sandeen announced to our entire class that there was no Santa Claus and our letters to Santa simply got thrown away. Walking

All Is Not Lost

home from school that day, I remember feeling not only stunned and let down, but also resentful, both about her presumption that we were old enough to know the truth, and that I had been deceived by the adults in my life. This, too, I never verbalized.

All through school, I never quite fit in. I was a Catholic kid living in a largely Baptist neighborhood, attending public school. On Saturdays I attended Catechism classes instead of getting to play with my friends. When I switched to Catholic school (fourth to ninth grades) I was still an outsider because these kids had been together since first grade. And being a mouthy, self-conscious, and rebellious child, I constantly got into trouble with the nuns (I was not a good girl). Transferring back to public school in the tenth grade was intimidating, going from a class of 30 to a student body of over 400.

My future was already sealed anyway, when, on my sixteenth birthday, I got pregnant, dropped out of

The Healing Journey

the eleventh grade, and got married. I was immediately ostracized from what few friends I had and expected to become an instant grownup. Still sixteen when my first child was born, I had my second at seventeen and my third at twenty.

When friends reminisce about summer camp or living in dorm rooms at college I have no idea what they are talking about. During those years I was busy changing diapers and running a household. I did return to high school when I was 23, but six weeks later, for the second time in my life I flunked algebra, and once again, dropped out. This was devastating.

My marriage was doomed. Though I had known my husband came from an abusive home I didn't know about the cycle of domestic abuse. Fortunately for both of us, the marriage ended before things got too extreme. I found a job that paid so little my kids and I were living at the poverty line. With no child support to augment my meager income, we struggled through three hard years. And then I had my moment of reckoning.

Like the substance abuser who must first admit there's a problem, one night, in a fit of misery, I had the revelation that until I accepted responsibility for the state of my life, I would remain stuck where I was. It was quite a moment, realizing that I and I alone was responsible for the choices I made in my life. This admission meant having to let go of the denial and blame that had been so much a part of my existence.

While this revelation was painful, difficult, and frightening, it was also empowering. I had taken my first step toward healing my tattered spirit and changing the direction of my life.

When people ask what it was that motivated me to change my life, the answer is easy. Misery was my first motivator. I didn't know what I wanted, but I knew I didn't want to hurt like this for the rest of my life.

This was when I discovered that getting rid of hurt requires pitching directly into it, exploring it, and then figuring out what to do. I learned that the peace of mind and happiness I so desperately wanted was like precious treasure buried beneath layers of muck that first had to be carefully and tediously cleared away. As we go through life, we are always much closer to our inner treasure than we realize. We just have to dig beneath the surface where it lies.

It took me years to recognize how much sadness (admittedly, much of it self imposed) I had experienced in my younger years. But by finally accepting where I was, taking responsibility for my choices and being willing to risk some kind of forward action, I was able to radically alter the course of my life.

Just so you know, there is nothing exceptional about me in terms of IQ or talent. I like to think that we all have unlimited potential and if we are willing to get past our fears and dig deep into our inner selves we will find a wealth of strength and capability. From there, it's what we choose to do with it.

All Is Not Lost

A Healing Step

Reviewing your history can give you perspective on how you view loss and hardship. Reflecting back on what you were consistently told as a child (or not told) can shed light on how you treat yourself when the chips are down. You also might gain some insights into your early fears and curiosities and how they manifest themselves now that you're a grownup. Or you can explore how old behavior patterns unknowingly created problems, as I did.

If you were a bothersome child like me, take comfort in knowing that the very traits and qualities that got you into trouble as a kid are same ones that help you succeed as an adult. My early curiosity (which my grandmother labeled as nosiness) helps me be an effective workplace consultant and writer. My loud voice and willingness to express myself (known as mouthiness when I was a kid) are assets in my speaking and that's how I have made my living since 1979.

My early rebelliousness connects to my value for independence, and gives me the confidence to live with the insecurities of self employment. In time, I discovered that my once burdensome qualities could work for me instead of against me. In other words, not all losses remain losses. You'll find the same in your life, now that you know how to look at your core qualities.

Spend some time thinking about how you got into trouble as a child and how those behaviors have helped stabilize your existence as you've grown up. These characteristics are the skills that help you handle challenge, loss or hardship. Treasure and cultivate them. They are the foundation of who you are, there to help you ease your burdens and work toward your dream. Even if your early years were difficult, in your history you will find the genesis of the core characteristics that have helped you get where you are.

Reviewing what was talked about or not talked

All Is Not Lost

about in your family can answer some questions about how you handle the uncomfortable areas of life. Make some conscious decisions about how you want to handle these subjects in your home instead of perpetuating old patterns. Maybe you'll reevaluate your children's most irritating behaviors and consider what positive characteristics these traits might develop into as they grow up.

For example, all of my kids had a (not so surprising) stubborn streak and I found myself sometimes admiring this quality. Though it was often obnoxious and inconvenient for me, I sensed that this tenacity would serve them well once they grew up. I was right.

Exploring your childhood losses may help you prevent some losses in your children's lives, or at least minimize them. If you have recently divorced, maybe you can more clearly recognize what your children are experiencing as they face conflicting loyalties and the complications of a new lifestyle. You may be more inclined to listen and less likely to talk them out of their feelings as some adults may have done with you.

Chapter 18
ANTICIPATORY GRIEF

Not all grief takes us off guard. Sometimes we cherish someone so much we worry that we may not survive their loss. I don't know anyone who has ever been more devoted to their mother than my own. My mom, the oldest of five children, adored her immigrant mother. As a child, I remember mom's frequent trips across town so she could spend time with her mother. Mondays they washed clothes in Grandma's wringer washer, Wednesdays they ironed, Fridays they shopped, and some Sundays we had dinner at Grandma's house.

My father, who went through a period of wanderlust, talked about moving to South America, California, Florida; anywhere but Michigan, where we lived. Mom refused, declaring that as long as her mother was alive, she wouldn't budge. But that wasn't all. Mom spent a lot of private time fretting about how lonely she would be if and when her mother died. She would cry at the mere thought.

For years, she wept over the fact that one day she would lose her mother. After all that crying, suffering, and worrying, mom tells me that when her mother did die, she never shed a tear. She had already done her grieving.

In a recent conversation with a woman I had just met, it came up that I was writing a book on loss and grief. The woman immediately told me about her aging dog who suffers from congestive heart failure and how she is already grieving the imminent loss of her pet. While the dog is sleeping in her lap, Joan's eyes will well with tears as she acknowledges the day is coming when she will no longer have the company of her beloved companion. She got very emotional just telling me about it.

When dad was diagnosed with colon cancer he was terribly ill. An intestinal blockage prevented him from being able to eat or drink for days. Severe anemia, pre-existing emphysema, and an esophageal stricture complicated his condition. The night before his surgery he was weak and could only talk in a whisper. There were six tubes attached to his body with liquids going in and liquids coming out.

Thinking this would be no different from his hip replacements and hernia operations, dad was eager to get this surgery over with and, in his words, "Get everything back on track." Every time he talked about getting well, going back to his part time job, or once again going out dancing with mom in a few weeks (they began dancing together as teens) I fought my tears.

Here was my father, gravely ill, talking about dancing again, and I knew he would never even make it through surgery. I was grateful for his poor eyesight so he couldn't see that I was fighting tears through most of our conversation. Somehow I managed to hold onto my composure until I reached my car, where I sat, sobbing for nearly an hour, grieving for dad, grieving for myself, and grieving for all of humanity over the sadness we must sometimes endure.

When my tears eased off, a feeling of calm swept over me and I felt a load lift from my shoulders. I think I must have taken the express line through the acceptance phase of grieving that night: I was ready for anything.

As things played out, dad made it through surgery but there was much to grieve over. He was never able to work again and he had to give up driving. To this day he and mom have not gone dancing, and he can no longer play his keyboard. A natural musician with near perfect pitch, dad started playing keyboard (by ear) in his late sixties. Every now and then he would give a command performance when I visited. He even gigged with a local band a few times; that's how good he was.

Maybe it was a mercy that my dad didn't realize treating cancer entailed far more than just a surgical procedure. Despite his going into remission, within a year's time, the disease and its treatment wasted him. He's still alive, but only shadow of who he was; weak though still mobile, pitifully thin and always cold, with his mind as compromised as his body. In a way I did lose my father, at least a good share of him.

My grief that night was intense and real. It helped me accept that things were about to drastically change for our family. It was one more example of how life only travels in one direction and you can't go back. I occasionally wonder if, when we bury dad, I will follow the example of mom and her mother. Maybe I've already shed the majority of my tears in anticipation of his death.

All Is Not Lost

A Healing Step

You may find yourself grieving the loss of a person or situation long before the final event and if you think this is a healthy outlet for your feelings, then do so. There may have been a time when I would have called anticipatory grieving an unnecessary stress, or self-induced pain. Now I think maybe it's simply preparation for the inevitable. Like many other things, it depends on the frequency and extent.

I bring this up because sometimes, when we take an action that is borne out of fear or dread, we can end up creating the very outcome we are trying to avoid. I remember a movie about a boy who was so convinced that the girl he loved would never go out with him that he did everything he could to shy away from her. She, of course, thought he couldn't stand her and therefore she wrote him off.

There is also the theory that whatever you put

in your mind and focus your energy on (be it a positive visualization or fearful thought), can set into motion the very circumstances that help bring it about. That's what the "visualize world peace" bumper stickers are all about. So it would be well to distinguish between anticipatory grieving, which is connected to reality, and runaway worry, a concoction of fear and fantasy. Given that the human mind is so creative and unruly, we probably do more of both than is necessary.

Anticipatory grief is one more example of the varied ways we approach loss and the many options available to us. We could say the one positive outcome of anticipating a loss is that the strength of your emotions can inspire you to consciously appreciate and savor what you have, for as along as you have it, and that's quite an achievement in itself.

All Is Not Lost

Chapter 19

ANGER AND ACCEPTANCE

When bad things happen, one of the many emotions we need to sort through is anger. If we become ill, we may get angry at ourself, our body, or even the doctor who diagnoses our condition. When a loved one dies, we might be angry at them for leaving us behind. A divorce can trigger a good deal of anger, especially if it involved betrayal or deception. We can get angry at life for being so harsh or cruel, or at God for allowing something so awful to happen. And with a little bit of creativity and perseverance, we can find a whole lot of other people to be mad at, too.

Elsewhere in this book I describe the anger I felt when my son was killed. It just didn't feel natural burying one of my children. Parents were supposed to die first, or even grandparents, all of whom, in our family, outlived their grandson by several years. You can imagine I was very angry over the unfairness of it all.

When I presented the minister with the elegy I had written for my son, I remember giving the poor man precise, insistent instructions on exactly how I wanted it read. I think he understood that I was so closed down with grief and outrage I didn't realize how I was behaving, nor did I care. My anger had to go somewhere.

Therapists and anger management counselors describe anger as a secondary emotion, stating that, while what is coming out of us may look, sound, and feel like anger, that's not really what it is. Fear, insecurity, and hurt are often expressed as anger, as are feelings of abandonment, frustration, and helplessness. For example, as couples in a troubled relationship approach the point of separation or divorce, much of their time is spent yelling, blaming, and venting their anger.

All Is Not Lost

I am suggesting that much of what they are expressing isn't really anger. They are grieving, but they just don't know it. Their anger is protecting them from their hurt.

I define anger as a defense mechanism that shields us from experiencing the full brunt of an emotion. In other words, people who keep themselves in a prolonged state of anger are wrapped in their "protections." They are closed down, shielded; in full defense mode. Temporarily, anger does us a service. It can keep us from having to feel the intensity of our grief or hurt until we have time to adjust and sort things out. But if we hold onto anger for too long, it can be our undoing.

As an individual more inclined toward anger than depression, I've since learned to look for the connecting point. That is, I want to know what root feeling is attached to my anger at the other end. If you find yourself feeling angry about something that's going on in your life, take a closer look and figure out what it's connected to. What presumptions did you have about life? What were your expectations? Did you think you were exempt from this kind of hurt? Were you thinking life would be fair? Well, it isn't. Life is exceedingly unfair.

It's unfair that people should die painful deaths, whether by illness or violence, and that our hearts or spirits sometimes end up broken by the very people we love. It's unfair that employers allow unhealthy, sometimes abusive work environments to exist, where people in subordinate positions are treated with disrespect, or where politics preside over principles. It's unfair that corporations can wantonly pollute our water, soil, and air and not have to clean it up or pay for it. It's unfair that some people have so much money that they blatantly waste, flaunt, or hoard it while others have so little they can barely subsist. It's unfair that children get cancer and diabetes, or are born with multiple disabilities. It's unfair that women and children and animals get abused in their homes. I could go on, but you get the point.

Life is unfair and getting angry won't stop the unfairness from happening. Life will go on whether we stay angry or not. If something terrible has happened to you, maybe you feel angry about being singled out. But remembering that anger is a secondary emotion can encourage you to discover what it's connected to. Go deeper. Then ask, why should you or I be exempt? It only takes a short look to regain perspective.

I think of my friend Mitchell, who, just a few years before the accident that paralyzed him, suffered burns so extensive that he lost his fingers and had to have his face rebuilt. Or my neighbor Ruth who buried a son and a daughter before either of them became full fledged adults. Then there are the families who lost someone on September 11.

We all have our losses to bear. Respecting the tragedies of others keeps me from feeling entitled; like

The Healing Journey

I'm so special that nothing bad should happen to me, or that I'm justified staying angry when it does. Life happens. Hurt happens. And we go on anyway.

We have to remind ourselves that the hard times help us truly connect with other human beings. It is our bond; our social glue. By trading anger for acceptance you'll find it easier to forgive, whether that means forgiving yourself or someone else. Once you accept what life is, instead of what you think it should be, or want it to be, you'll find the place of peace you've been looking for, and more.

A Healing Step

If, in your grief, you have been closed down with anger and you're ready to give it up, you have some work to do (if you're not ready to give it up you have even more work to do). Your first step is in facing up to the fact that you are a human being, living in a neutral world where things you consider bad, hurtful, or unfortunate will happen, most of which are beyond the realm of your control. I'm sorry, but that's the way it is. Next, accept that, even though in many ways you are a very special person, this does not mean you are exempt from heartache or conflict in your relationships, unjust treatment by your employer, nor are you and those you love necessarily immune to illness, turmoil, or injury.

Getting angry and blaming people, circumstances, or even God for bad things that happen to you will only increase and perpetuate your anxiety. In directing blame (responsibility) toward any source other than yourself, you are, in effect, relinquishing control. If you in no way contributed to this situation your option is to accept, not resist. If you had even a remote hand in helping make it happen, own up.

Wishing, hoping, blaming or getting angry over the way things are will not change the circumstances, nor will any of these resistances prevent more bad things from happening. However, they will keep you closed down, meaning that you'll be unable to fully participate in your life.

Perhaps it's occurred to you that these declarations reflect the sentiment found in the Serenity Prayer and you're right. These statements also parallel the work of Dr. Albert Ellis and his model of Rational Emotive Therapy (RET), a powerful approach to personal transformation. I highly recommend his many books, especially *A Guide To Rational Living.*

One last thing I will ask you to accept is that you have tremendous potential for creating a life of fulfillment and much of your serenity will come from your ability to openly accept all of life's experiences, not just the ones that feel good or make you happy.

All Is Not Lost

Chapter 20
AGING AND ILLNESS

Illness and aging can trigger a sense of loss and even an extended grieving process, depending on the extent to which one's capacity is compromised. Good self care, monitoring, and careful health maintenance can prevent, or at least postpone the inevitable aches and pains that often accompany aging. Regardless of your age, if you feel any new sensations or symptoms, make sure you check them out.

Certainly, aging or illness involve the process of letting go, or simply the acknowledgment that we are slowly losing ground. I speak with some authority here as I approach a birthday that signals the beginning of my sixties. So far, so good, but I know (and so does my body) that I'm not a twenty year old anymore.

The Healing Journey

As we age, if we've enjoyed an active lifestyle, at some point we will be confronted with the issue of slowing down. Maybe we can't run or walk as many miles as we once did, or as fast. Maybe a sports injury or chronic condition interferes with our ability to stay at the top of our game. Depending on our fitness level and capabilities, at some point we may mourn some of our lost capacity, whether it's a slow, gradual decline or the rapid worsening of an infirmity.

There's a line where illness and aging intersect. It's hard to find an extended family who hasn't had to contend with cancer, heart disease, osteoporosis, arthritis, stroke, diabetes, Alzheimer's or dementia. As my mother often says, "Aging is not for the faint hearted." Of course, not all of life's losses can be prevented, but a consistent program of healthy practices can make a difference. So can attitude.

Although they've done an okay job of taking care of themselves, one major difference between my parents' attitudes toward health and mine is the question of sharing responsibility for medical diagnosis and treatment.

Having conducted stress management seminars for nearly two decades I've learned quite a bit about wellness and health maintenance and it has worked in my favor. But my parents put far more faith in their doctors and the medical system than I do. If they like their physician, they dispense with a second opinion.

When I see what arthritis has done to my mother's hands I want to weep. Because she, like dad, is not inclined to complain, I didn't know how incapacitated she had become until a few months ago when she showed me her hands and I felt a stab of guilt that I had never noticed. Ironically, her acceptance of this condition (the same acceptance, by the way, that I've been harping about through this entire book) has been her undoing.

Instead of rallying against this disease and actively seeking out a specialist who may have been able to help, my mother has accepted a series of largely ineffective treatments prescribed by her general practitioner. I am now, in the eleventh hour, insisting that she see a specialist. In my inexhaustible quest for unearthing life's lessons wherever I go, mom's situation has taught me that a blanket acceptance about everything that happens in life is as ineffective as a blanket rejection.

This is also a perfect time for me to state that when I use the term acceptance I don't mean a generalized passivity to all that happens. Acceptance is the ability to actively sort out the rational truths in a situation, explore your options, and respond appropriately.

I am reminded of my friend Chuck who was diagnosed with throat cancer last year. The first physician told him the cancer could be removed, but Chuck would lose half of his face. Deciding to not accept this grim option, he got a second opinion. Today, thanks to his persistence, a successful clinical trial, and the unrelenting support of his wife Josie and their friends, he is cancer free. Chuck says the best part is that he can smile about it because his face is still intact.

My friend Eddie nearly died because his primary care physician misdiagnosed his condition. A sigmoidoscopy failed to detect colon cancer and instead of doing more tests and trying to figure out why this forty year old man was in so much pain and experiencing periodic bleeding, the doctor rather curtly told Eddie he should "do something about his stress." Fortunately, my friend changed physicians in time to get a correct diagnosis and treatment that saved his life.

One of my clients, as he neared retirement, made frequent comments about how much he hated getting older. This man mourned for the old days when he didn't have to cope with aches and pains. But he also resisted the idea of a healthier diet or physical maintenance such as yoga, stretching, or strengthening exercises to help his aging body feel less creaky. This man's refusal to help himself was a reminder of the needless pain we inflict on ourselves through our own resistance; that when we refuse to accept what is, we end up getting stuck in the very place we don't want to be.

Yes, an aging body requires a little more maintenance, but what are the alternatives? I'd rather spend a few minutes stretching and strengthening my body than complaining about not feeling so hot. How about you?

❦

A Healing Step

Perhaps aging or illness simply aren't issues for you yet, and if that's the case, I'll simply encourage you to take good care of yourself so you can do what you enjoy for as long as possible. Take especially good care of yourself in times of stress or crisis. Be religious about your medical screenings. Know your resting and active pulse, your blood type, and cholesterol numbers. Engage in some kind of regular exercise to keep your physical self fit. Eat a moderately healthy diet.

Get to know your body and pay attention to signs or symptoms that something is going on (periods of anxiety or low energy, frequent headaches, localized pain or discomfort that doesn't go away). Don't rely on over the counter medicines if your symptoms persist.

If you get sick, especially if it's a serious illness, get a second opinion and do your own research. Talk with others, use the Internet, read books, and even medical texts so you can gain a quick education about what's going on with your body. You may need to be very persistent, but the good news is that the information is out there.

It all comes down to this: you can complain about getting older but that will only make you feel worse. You can grouse about not feeling so hot but you may be ignoring something that needs attention. Or you can pledge to be the diligent caretaker of your mental, physical, and spiritual well-being.

The Healing Journey

The reality is that aging brings with it the possibility of illness and some isolated infirmities but you can actively participate in the maintenance of your health, keeping yourself as happy, healthy, and vital as possible. I hope this is an option you can live with.

Chapter 21

DISAPPOINTMENT AND LETDOWN

One of my friends just told me her younger son is out of control, using drugs, stealing to pay for them, and lying to cover up for his actions. This is a heartbreak many parents experience. Lest anyone think this woman failed as a parent, her older son is a model citizen: responsible, self-motivated, and an earnest, achieving student.

Somewhere in the scheme of things, regardless

of our environment, we human beings make choices that can affect the whole of our lives. Sometimes kids who seem to have everything end up killing themselves or sacrificing their futures, while others rise above a poverty stricken, dangerous, drug-filled climate to achieve far more than the average.

Having raised two teenagers (my eldest son moved in with his father after finishing ninth grade) I remember the rebellious periods Cathy and Robbie went through. It's frustrating to see someone you love taking chances, experimenting with alcohol, drugs, and sex. Knowing my own history, I was sometimes surprised (and relieved) my kids didn't put me through the same hell storm of defiance I gave my own mom.

Children don't always match our expectations. By expectations I mean that we want the best for our kids and if possible, we would like to shield them from self-inflicted pain. When we try to influence our children, they often get defensive, telling us they can take care of themselves and why don't we just stay out of their business. When we try to explain that they could do better, kids often think we're saying they aren't good enough.

Proper discipline; that is, structure and rules combined with empathy and understanding go a long way in guiding kids through the toughest time of their lives, but some of them will still make bad decisions, regardless of our efforts.

As I talked with a woman whose fifteen year old son was murdered, she had additional grief to cope with. At the time her son was killed, her thirteen year old daughter had been living on the streets for nearly a year. After repeated attempts to control her daughter's behavior this beleaguered mother quit fighting because it was doing more harm than good. After her daughter left home, contact was infrequent and filled with conflict.

But the mother knew she had exhausted all of

her options; the time had come to let go. Yes, she was afraid that her daughter was gone and lost forever. She says she had to accept that cold reality. In time, the daughter gave up her street life, but it was tough going for a while.

There's a reverse side to the family portrait, too. I know a young man whose parents were so caught up in their own egos and personal issues they kicked him out of the house when he was only sixteen. On his own, this disheartened youth found a job and an apartment, so he could continue attending high school. I am astounded at Craig's resilience, sense of responsibility, and capacity to accept being so different from his peers at such a tender age. Contrary to what one might expect, his apartment was not a site for parties and bashes. Friends came over, but alcohol wasn't allowed at his place.

Craig was fixed on survival, and his perseverance paid off. Despite periods where he had no home to call his own, where he worked in a succession of unconventional jobs, and grappled with daily uncertainty, Craig, now 25, is a remarkable individual who did an outstanding job of raising himself. This bright, personable, and enterprising young man now faces a brilliant and promising future.

I also know a young woman who, due to the lack of guidance in her home, began "parenting" herself while still an adolescent. She has grown into an exceptionally well balanced individual and high achiever who has a remarkable capacity for self-awareness and self-evaluation.

Both of these young adults impress me with their common sense and self-governance at such early ages. With their lack of parental influence they could have made drastically different choices. Think of the obstacles they had to overcome and the forgiveness they've needed to exercise. Somehow, they knew it would not serve them to stay angry at their parents for not living up to their expectations.

All Is Not Lost

Once again (perhaps you felt it coming) we cycle back to the subject of letting go. We cannot control the behavior of those we love or force them to live the way we think they should. We cannot impose "good" choices on another and it does no good to wish for that kind of power. We can pray. We can simply do our best.

We may first use empathy and understanding, and then logic. When that doesn't work, we may try threats or ultimatums, and they may not work, either. We may opt for counseling. We may, out of sheer desperation, escalate to detention, incarceration, or other disciplinary options.

Sometimes these measures help and sometimes they don't. It's hard having to accept that perhaps all we can do is back off and allow the situation to run its course. Sometimes there is actually more control in letting go than there is in exercising force. When we don't give others anything to push against, they might let up because there's nothing to resist.

The Healing Journey

Let me describe one of my early lessons in letting go. I enjoy using this example in my presentations because not only can people immediately relate, but they also recognize that this concept has universal applications. Having been born and raised in the Midwest, I learned to drive through winter storms on snowy, slippery roads. Initially, this made me very tense and my instinctive reaction was to grasp the steering wheel in a tense, vise like grip. Little did I realize this was the exact opposite of what was most effective.

After demonstrating my fierce hold on the steering wheel, I like to ask audience members if this technique gave me more control or less control over my vehicle. They always say less. When I ask what I needed to do so I could gain more control over my car, they tell me I needed to relax and let go. They're right.

In theory, this principle is easy to grasp, but it's hard to put into practice. We may know, deep down, that we need to relax or let go instead of clutch, threaten, or force, but it's terribly difficult to do so. This is what "tough love" is all about.

When people we love do things that hurt or worry us and intervention hasn't worked, sometimes our best option is to back off and let go rather than cut off all ties. This isn't rejection and it isn't giving up. It's simply waiting for the person we care about to come around. It's living day to day with hurt, worry, and concern in the background while we attempt to live life as fully as possible. No, this isn't ideal, nor are there any guarantees. But our job is to simply do the best we can, then wait and see.

❦

A Healing Step

People will let you down. Of course, it's especially painful and difficult when it's your child, but sometimes that's the only way they can learn their lessons. You cannot always protect loved ones from hurt or danger. Without playing the rescuer, try to leave the door open; better to let someone go while you still have love in your heart than to push them away with contempt.

What follows is living one day at a time, and by holding out and hoping for the best you can at least move forward with your life. Truth be told, people are free to make their own choices and take their own risks, including our children.

Life constantly exposes us to circumstances that require us to let go, and the options are not risk free. From the moment when, as a toddler, you risked letting go of a safe support to take your first shaky baby steps, to the day you relinquish directing the steps in someone else's life, you will often be faced with the choice of letting go.

If you have the need, find a support group, a dependable listening ear, or a therapist to help you through the initial heartache. Then step back and let life unfold as it will.

All Is Not Lost

Chapter 22
GIVE AND TAKE

We are all familiar with the words, "The Lord giveth and the Lord taketh away." There is certainly a ring of truth to this bittersweet reminder. I say bittersweet because times of heartache also bring unexpected gifts that would not happen under any other circumstances.

I recently talked with two sisters whose parents died within a year of each other. Although both women were well into their thirties when they lost their parents, they spoke of feeling orphaned and abandoned. But it wasn't long before the older sister assumed the role of matriarch in the family. She said it was as if an internal switch got tripped, and to the relief and appreciation of her siblings, she rose to the occasion.

The Healing Journey

While speaking with a man who had just emerged from what he described as the most difficult, trying period in his life, he marveled over the support he received from his friends and family. Mike was both taken off guard and deeply touched by how much people cared. He said the outpouring of empathy and concern was something he never would have predicted and had this bad period in his life not happened, he'd never have known how blessed he was.

After making that statement, Mike paused, shook his head, and a look of amazement washed over his face. He smiled, adding how odd it seemed to reflect on his trauma with such gratitude.

This reminded me of the support I received when Robbie died and how it helped me be more compassionate when clients or friends of mine experience a loss. Emotional support, much like a hug, feels good both in the giving and receiving.

People my age whose parents, like mine, are still

All Is Not Lost

alive, are finding that it's now our turn to give back. Many of us are beginning to at least keep a watchful eye on our aging parents, and others are heavily involved in various types of caregiving. For those of us who haven't been particularly close to our parents in the past, we can now gain a broader perspective of them and ourselves.

For my mother's eightieth birthday I made her a memory book. Not only did I ask family members and friends to send old photos, I also asked them to write a favorite memory about Julie. The photos were great but the stories were by far my favorites and one of the most often mentioned comments was that mom could stand on her head (unassisted) until well in her sixties.

The hours and weeks I spent planning and working on the memory book were nothing in comparison to what I got back, like learning that my mother is unanimously known by her friends and family as someone who never says a bad word about others.

Our world is moving so fast these days, it's hard enough taking time for ourselves, let alone others, even those we care about. Yet if tragedy strikes, no matter how busy or overloaded we are, we find the time to deal with it.

One woman I know, an only child, took the time to visit her mother in a nursing home for nearly two decades, maintaining a regular visitation schedule even though her mother became withdrawn and unresponsive the last few years before her death. Janie would put cute accessories on her mother to encourage more attention from the staff. She would also constantly rub, touch, and carry on a one-sided conversation, just in case her mother could hear her or feel her presence.

After my friend Antoinette survived a brain aneurism and I visited her in the hospital, I was warmed to see her surrounded by so many gifts. What loving friends she has, and she deserves them.

All Is Not Lost

Sometimes, as in the Buddhist faith, judgmental words such as "bad" or "good" just don't fit a situation, because while it was unfortunate Antoinette had the stroke, the outpouring of love and support she continues to receive is something you'd never want to take back from her.

Divorce, too, has its own give and take. One couple I know have made much better friends than they did spouses, and splitting up improved their parenting, too. In the case of partners who finally decide to formally end a relationship long since over, there can come a sense of relief and release along with the sadness. After years of feeling emotionally stifled it is freeing to end the denial and rationalization that become so much a part of one's life when all is not well.

Even though my divorce happened many years ago, I remember feeling less lonely once I was on my own than I had through the last years of my marriage. Living with someone who is unable or unwilling to meet your needs feels terribly lonely and lacking. Being free of their emotional remoteness gives you room to reclaim your wholeness once you're on you own, and that's quite a gift.

My friend Mary suffered a home fire last year. This was not a little grease fire that ruins the drapes and causes smoke damage throughout the house. No, this was a total loss, life-threatening fire that claimed the family cat. They narrowly escaped, managing to save their dog and what they were wearing. Instead of expressing bitterness over the unfairness of not being able to do even a quick sweep of cherished possessions, Mary is grateful to be alive and well.

Having survived cancer seven years ago, Mary's illness changed the way she and her husband live. They began directing their energy toward family and friends instead of their careers, finding less demanding jobs and cutting back on school and business activities. Their commitment to staying connected was certainly evident to local police and firefighters who were overwhelmed at the number of people who showed up to offer help and support. Mary says if the fire had happened seven years ago it would have been a different story.

Convinced that you get what you give, Mary is quick to express appreciation for what she has instead of focusing on the losses or misfortune in her life. She put it all in perspective by telling me, "Possessions can be replaced, but beloved people and pets cannot."

Those of us who are pet owners grieve mightily when we lose our companions and we are willing to go through staggering expense and inconvenience to keep an ailing pet alive. I know someone who refinanced her home to pay vet bills so she could treat her aging horse's ailments the last two years of his life. Another woman I know took a week off work so she could attend to her dying dog's every need, right up to the end.

Two summers ago my horse, Ladiebug, whom I shamelessly dote on, somehow got a piece of loose fence wire wrapped around her right hind leg. In the struggle to free herself, she tore a huge gaping hole in the front of her joint. Although the wound was large and deep, the veterinarian assured me that there was no nerve or joint damage and that she would heal, given time and proper treatment.

It's heartbreaking when children or pets are hurt because there's no way to explain why they must endure their pain. My horse, accustomed to spending her days and nights outdoors at will, was confined to a 12 by 12 stall for five weeks.

For those who say there are no coincidences, a break in my usually busy speaking schedule allowed me to be with her every day those first five weeks. I talked to her, brushed, petted, massaged, and fed her. Sometimes I just sat in her stall. She seemed to understand this was a time to be quiet (not all horses do). Finally I was able to take her out for short grazes and then, brief walks.

All Is Not Lost

After six weeks we graduated to the pasture. This was the moment. When I released her would she leap or run and reinjure herself like so many horses do? Her leg was still heavily bandaged and the healing had weeks to go. I released the lead line and stood back, holding my breath.

Ladiebug stood for a moment, looking around as if in disbelief. She was free. No rope, no walls. She stood like a statue, and then did what she does almost every day of her life. She dropped to the ground and began to roll in the grass. But it wasn't just a roll. My mare shut her eyes and rubbed her head against the earth. And then she moaned; a deep, long, guttural sound that seemed to release everything she had so stoically held inside for so many weeks.

Ladiebug rolled from one side to the other and back again, still moaning, still delightfully rubbing her head against the grass. I watched and sobbed. Then she got up, shook herself, walked a few steps and started

The Healing Journey

grazing. I now knew we would make it.

The rehabilitation was slow and the medical treatment taxing. During those months I learned about wrapping and debriding a wound; something I never want to do again. And I learned patience. We lost a year of our training for the show ring but we gained a bond we never could have achieved in any other way. As Ladiebug continued to heal, my dad began complaining about not feeling well.

Dad's illness has brought our family closer together. My two brothers and I are happy to spend our time, money, and energy to help mom and dad in whatever way we can. We each bring our separate strengths, personalities, and perspectives and it makes for a pretty good mix.

Bob slips mom shopping money whenever he visits. I accompanied mom and dad to oncologist appointments back when the chemo began and still help with doctor visits and assorted chores. And Steve has

All Is Not Lost

surely won himself extra points in heaven because he has spent one night a week at mom and dad's house for well over a year. His wonderful wife Cindy hasn't minded a bit. In fact, she encourages it.

For me, the biggest "gift", if I may call it that, coming from dad's illness has been discovering my mother. As a child I competed with my brothers for dad's attention. Mom was always just there, in the background. Dad, Bob, Steve and I were the performers and she was our audience of one.

In the past eighteen months I've spent more time with my mother than ever in the past and she's quite a woman. Mom is the one in the family who changes the screens, mows the lawn, and does minor home repairs. She has a small alterations business with a devoted clientele, including me. Shortly before dad started feeling poorly, my eighty year old mom started talking about wanting a computer, so I bought her an iMac just like mine.

The Healing Journey

At first it seemed like such bad timing, but logging time on her computer while dad is resting has been a Godsend. I am her computer coach and she is an eager student, going online, visiting web sites, making her own greeting cards, playing virtual pool or bowling with Steve, and staying in daily touch with me via e-mail whether I'm home or traveling.

In watching my mother tackle her caregiver challenges, I now know where my resourcefulness comes from. If dad hadn't gotten sick I never would have realized how much she and I have in common. Give and take.

If the world (or I) were perfect, I would have made these discoveries under more pleasant circumstances, but I am grateful to have gotten so well acquainted with the woman who gave birth to me. I am in awe of her energy and positive outlook, especially now, as the bulk of her days centers around caregiving. She does not whine or complain, nor does she cry for help.

All Is Not Lost

And as her devoted daughter I try to relieve and rescue her before that would be necessary.

❧

A Healing Step

When things seem so grim and hopeless there is often a glimmer of light somewhere; a promise of a better, more peaceful time. This is one small strand of comfort you can hold onto, if or when you find yourself in a cold, lonely place. Something will happen, someone will be there, and you might just be surprised how it all unfolds. Maybe there are no coincidences.

If you are in a position where caregiving has become one of your responsibilities or you know someone who has transitioned into this position, I recommend *A Caregivers Journey* by Karen Twichell. This book can be a haven for those who find themselves in this demanding, unrelenting, and sometimes unrewarding role.

The Healing Journey

If you are facing a loved one's terminal illness and you want a hopeful, helpful perspective, I also recommend *Final Gifts*. Sensitively written by Maggie Callanan and Patricia Kelley, two hospice nurses, this book touched my heart innumerable times and helped me learn that even in dying we can still give gifts to ourselves as well as those we love. I do not, however, recommend reading it on an airplane, as I did, where I wept from Michigan to California. It is a touching book.

Despite our miracles of technology and high standard of living, or maybe because of them, it's easy to forget how simple life really is; that all we really want, or need, is to be loved, to feel important, and to make a difference in our own way. In the midst of crisis, if you were to sit down and make a list of everything that's important to you, chances are your list would be very, very short.

When we venture close to the edge of death (our own, or accompanying someone else on their journey) we find a gift—the almost blinding clarification about what we truly want out of life. From there, it's taking the steps to make it happen.

Chapter 23
HOPE AND PROGRESS

We don't see the grass as it grows but one day we look out at the lawn and realize it needs mowing again. The progression of healing is equally hard to measure, perhaps because grief recedes more slowly than grass grows. But there's a day when you suddenly realize you don't hurt as much.

Maybe you hear yourself laugh or tell someone you're fine, or even great, where up to this point you simply wouldn't have said anything. Your mood takes you by surprise so you do a quick self assessment, noticing that the parts of your mind and body that had recently felt so fragile and broken are beginning to mend. The gap has widened between you and the pain you were in, and you don't even know when it happened.

You didn't notice anything when you woke up this morning, or yesterday, or the day before, but you feel different. This is how it happens. The process of healing is slow, subtle, and invisible, but all of a sudden it reaches critical mass, and, for the first time, you can measure some of the distance between where you started and where you are now. It's quite a feeling.

No one can hand us a calendar of the month's grief events or predict how long the process will take. Suffice to say that at some point, the hellhole of pain you initially floundered in is no longer as deep or wide as it once was, nor the sides as steep. You indeed, have made progress, just like everyone said you would.

But you've felt bad for so long that how you feel right now is almost foreign, unfamiliar. There are new questions to consider. Is it okay to feel this way? Does this mean you're forgetting your loved one or being unfaithful to their memory? Does feeling so separate from your ex mean you never really cared? Is this new feeling of lightness a good thing? Is it bad?

It all just is. You have progressed to a new place in your healing. Your heart and mind are mending. You have progressed to a point where you never thought you'd be again and you'll have new things to work on now. You still have further to go, but the hardest part is over.

You're preparing to leave the land of the grieving behind and venture back into the land of the living. You don't have to hurry, and your journey isn't over. You will still come back to the grieving place from time to time when you need to, and maybe sometimes when you don't want to. But things are different now. They're not as bad. And no, you won't forget your loved one. You are not being unfaithful. You are not cold hearted. You are simply moving on.

The Healing Journey

Maybe you have not yet reached this pivotal point in your healing journey but you will. Have faith and trust that wherever you are right now is where you need to be. We've discussed that grief is something you cannot rush. If you try to hurry it, your hurt will express itself in other ways.

Healing takes time and the progress you're making, just like the growing grass, doesn't show until all of a sudden. Be patient. It will come to pass and there will be a moment when you know. If you have not yet progressed beyond your deep hurt, what I'm describing is how you will feel once you have gained a foothold in your healing. Let the knowledge that it will come bolster your faith and give you hope.

A Healing Step

Somewhere along the healing journey you'll have that moment of revelation that signals you've reached the other side of your grief. You will feel a sweet, odd wash of awareness, both in the absence of the familiar, gnawing ache that filled your soul, and the presence of a foreign lightness you haven't felt in so long. It's quite a moment. Savor it.

If you're so inclined, dare to venture forward in time, projecting your thoughts toward the place of peace you're sampling, and think about what this means. Now project backward, to the recent time when all you knew was hurt and measure how far you've come. Bring yourself back to the present.

I have stated in several ways that you can emerge from your loss a new and different person. As you hover between the place of pain and freedom from it, you will find new parts of yourself. Pay attention. Before this awareness goes away, review what you felt, what you thought, and how you helped yourself get to where you are right now.

Take the time to reflect on what you've been

through because, before you know it, the sharpness of your pain will fade, as will the keenness of the realizations you've had along the way. You want to capture as much of the learning as possible before it goes away.

It's time to collect what you've discovered about yourself and life, the people around you, and especially your insights and spiritual lessons. You're on the brink of reentering your old world, but it's really a new world if you want it to be.

You have the chance to live your life with more depth, sensitivity, and conviction. Your heart and soul that felt so empty not long ago, are beginning to fill again. You have taken enough steps in the healing journey where you can look back and view the other side of your grief. Look how far you've come. Your new life awaits you when you're ready, and right now you have no idea how far you can go.

All Is Not Lost

Chapter 24

YOUR OWN GROUND ZERO

Following September 11 the phrase "ground zero" fell into common usage. I had never heard the term before, and living so far away from the devastation, it was impossible for me to fully comprehend what actually living near a ground zero truly meant. My visit to Washington DC in early October took care of that.

The atmosphere was completely different than at home. The mood was somber. The topic of the attacks came up everywhere I went, even during consumer transactions. Everyone was conscious of what had happened; of what could still happen.

At some point in our lives we all face crisis; our own personal ground zero. Colossal loss or emotional devastation drives us to the core of all that we believe and gives us the impetus to more clearly express it in thought and action. When crisis occurs, we may at first be stunned with shock, denial, or incomprehension, unable to fully process the reality. But let me restate, it's during this same delicate period that our hearts and minds momentarily open, exposing that deep, private part of ourselves we may not even know exists.

Crisis opens us up, offering insight that can only be accessed in times of emergency. Like storm clouds momentarily parting in a darkened sky, we catch a quick glimpse of the light within us. Surprising thoughts converge and instantly crystallize. In this flash of enlightenment we make private promises, pledging to live more fully, love more deeply, show more appreciation, forgive our grudges, or take things less for granted.

What were your immediate thoughts when you first heard about, or saw the unbelievable images of our national crisis? What private vows did you make and have you kept them? Your immediate thoughts and declarations following this tragedy, or any extreme personal trauma, constitute a message from your inner self about what is really important to you.

Take heed. This was your wisdom speaking. Maybe you reflected on things you've been neglecting or putting off, or you had an immediate shot of regret over something you had taken for granted. Maybe you counted your blessings. Only you know. And only you can act upon your wisdom of the moment. Don't let it disappear. Let it be your guide.

Several times in this book I've stated that life is uncertain. While this is something we know intellectually, we only get it at a gut level after experiencing crisis or loss. But pain and anguish fade with time and despite your personal promises, you could lapse back into old patterns unless you make conscious decisions about how you want to live from here on out. To transform your life, periodically revisit what you've learned from crisis. That's how you make the lessons last.

The Healing Journey

A Final Healing Step

September 11 was a crisis we shared as a nation, and for some it was a life altering wake up call. You can use any personal crisis as a watershed event if you are willing to visit your own ground zero. This involves asking, and answering, some penetrating questions. Below you will find a sample of such questions and maybe you'll create some additional ones of your own.

What kind of person were you before your moment of reckoning? What were you taking for granted? Following your crisis, what were your immediate thoughts, promises, and regrets? As a result of the immediate reflections and oaths you made at that pivotal moment, how are you different today?

Consciously monitor your behavior at home, at work, with loved ones and friends. Think about how you are different now. Consider what it says about you

All Is Not Lost

if there are no significant changes after you've faced a defining moment. But consider what it says about you if you have! Conscientious people tend to emerge from bad situations with a renewed commitment to live better and make things better.

In the blink of an eye our world can change. It could be good or bad, but there's always something to be learned; something our inner wisdom will unearth. Whenever you are a faced with a crisis or life changing event, consider that you've been handed the challenge of a lifetime; *your* lifetime.

Turn inward to your core and follow the light that shines from the wise part of you. It will keep you on the path. Deciding to live a more reflective life not only prepares you for crisis, it also allows you to more fully experience joyful times such as a birth, spiritual awakening, marriage (sometimes even a divorce), a new relationship, or personal achievement.

Such insightful living also helps you plan for

the end. It helps you conceive how you will live and maybe even die. Complete a living will. Let your family know your preferences about organ donations and whether or not you desire extreme or heroic measures to keep you alive. Let it be known if you prefer cremation or burial and what kind of memorial service you desire. Taking care of these details now will make it much easier on those you leave behind.

Keeping the end in mind, take time to consider how you will leave your mark on the world and how you want people to talk about you after you're gone. This won't happen by accident. Once you identify what you want said about you, immediately start living that way. Let the inevitability of your passing translate into consciously planning how you will live the rest of your days, with quality, compassion, and ongoing enrichment. I hope in some small way, you'll begin today.

All Is Not Lost

AFTERWORD

Writing *All Is Not Lost* was a journey in itself because it came as such a surprise. Ideas spilled out of me long before I realized I had a book in progress, but the more I wrote, the more there was to say.

As I told people the title of this book, they spoke of their own losses. In the six months since I began this project, several of my friends have experienced crises or traumas of their own, and some of their stories appear in this book.

While this subject could fill volumes, I had to stop somewhere. I do hope, however, that even if I didn't address the specific situation you're grappling with, you still found ideas and concepts to help ease your hurt.

As the author of this book, I found comfort in writing it. If there was anything within these pages you have found particularly comforting, or you would like to share your own healing journey, please feel free to contact me.

❧

ABOUT THE AUTHOR

A lifelong Lansing area resident, Leslie Charles lives on a four acre wildlife preserve with her partner Rob. An award winning professional speaker with expertise in the subjects of stress and change management, customer service, and communication, she established her company TRAININGWORKS in 1979.

For information about inviting Leslie to address your organization or association, call 517.675.7535 or visit www.lesliecharles.com or send an E-mail to leschas@aol.com. You can review excerpts from her critically acclaimed book *Why is Everyone So Cranky?* at www.whyiseveryonesocranky.com.

LESLIE'S BOOKS & PRODUCTS

All Is Not Lost	$11.95
Why Is Everyone So Cranky?	$12.95
The Customer Service Companion	$10.95
The Companion Study Guide	$6.95
Stick To It!	$11.95
The Instant Trainer	$17.95

Memory Bracelets: Wearable Remembrance
"Jewelry For The Rest Of Us"

The memory bracelet is a meaningful and attractive accessory worn in commemoration of a loved one now gone, making a wonderful gift for yourself or someone you care about. Each bracelet is made to your specifications.

For details on Leslie's products please visit:
www.LeslieCharles.com
www.WhyIsEveryoneSoCranky.com
www.HealingGriefandLoss.com
www.WearableRemembrance.com

You may also order directly from **Yes!Press.**
Please include your name, address, and phone with payment. Shipping is $4.00. Leslie will be happy to personalize your books; just include the desired names.

Yes!Press

PO Box 956 • East Lansing, MI 48826 • 517.675.7535